lonely

POCKET

AMSTERDAM

TOP EXPERIENCES · LOCAL LIFE

CATHERINE LE NEVEZ

Contents

Plan Your Trip 4

Clogs
ANDRII MALKOV/SHUTTERSTOCK ©

Welcome to Amsterdam

Amsterdam showcases its heritage in its charming canal architecture, museums filled with works by Old Masters, *jenever* (Dutch gin) tasting houses and candlelit *bruin cafés* (traditional Dutch pubs). Yet this free-spirited city is also forging a future focused on sustainability, and is a multinational melting pot with an incredible diversity of cultures and cuisines, along with some of Europe's hottest nightlife venues, in a compact, village-like setting.

Leidsegracht (p70)
FOOTAGECLIPS/SHUTTERSTOCK

Amsterdam's Top Experiences

COLORMAKER/SHUTTERSTOCK ©

Admire art at the Rijksmuseum (p98)

COLORX/SHUTTERSTOCK ©

See the work of a master at the Van Gogh Museum (p102)

Glimpse the annexe behind the diary at Anne Frank Huis (p62)

DARRYL BROOKS/SHUTTERSTOCK ©

Explore Museum Rembrandthuis (p146)

Marvel at the opulence of the Koninklijk Paleis (p42)

Wander through Vondelpark (p106)

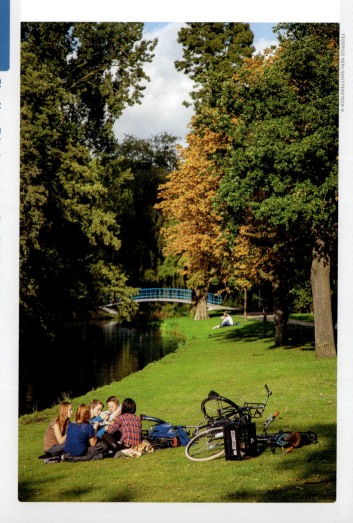

FEDERICO NERY/SHUTTERSTOCK ©

Discover world cultures at the Wereldmuseum Amsterdam (p134)

Visit Amsterdam's oldest building, the Oude Kerk (p44)

Dining Out

Multinational Amsterdam's sizzling-hot food scene features a cornucopia of cuisines from around the globe, as well as classic Dutch snacks, re-invented traditional recipes, on-trend establishments pioneering world-first concepts, sustainable eateries (often vegetarian or vegan) and wine, cocktail and craft-beer pairings.

Dutch Cuisine

Traditional Dutch cuisine revolves around meat, potatoes and vegetables. Typical dishes include *stamppot* (pictured) – potatoes mashed with another vegetable (usually kale or endive) and served with smoked sausage and strips of bacon.

But fresh winds are blowing through the traditional Dutch kitchen, adding contemporary twists to centuries-old recipes.

Current Trends

Sustainability and plant-based menus are driving Amsterdam's food revolution. Concept restaurants are popping up all over the city, and gourmet street food and all-day brunch are big. Foodhallen (p116), in the De Hallen tram depot-turned-cultural complex, has a host of eateries and is a fantastic place to take the city's dining temperature.

Best Traditional Dutch

Bistro Amsterdam Dutch classics. (p72)

Van Dobben Meaty goodness, diner-style. (p88)

Pantry A *gezellig* (cosy, convivial) atmosphere and honest Dutch fare. (p90)

Hap Hmm Homey, heart-warming Dutch comfort food. (p111)

Best Contemporary Dutch

De Silveren Spiegel Refined Dutch cuisine in a romantic step-gabled townhouse. (p51)

Wilde Zwijnen Creative multicourse menus in a rustic-industrial setting. (p139)

Pompstation Premium Dutch produce in a 1912 pumphouse. (p139)

Gebr Hartering In a seductive canal-side location; the

AS FOODSTUDIO/SHUTTERSTOCK ©

menu changes daily but is unfailingly delicious. (p156)

Best Vegan

Bonboon Elevated vegan cuisine. (p72)

Mediamatic ETEN Produce is grown in on-site greenhouses. (p157)

Vegan Junk Food Bar Plant-based burgers and vegan 'ribs' at several locations. (p90)

Best Budget

Le Salonard Satisfying gourmet sandwiches and wines by the glass. (p125)

Sterk Staaltje Hearty, lovingly prepared deli items like soups, salads and fantastic sandwiches. (p156)

Vleminckx Slather your golden *frites* (fries) in mayonnaise, curry or myriad other sauces. (p50)

De Laatste Kruimel Sweet treats and fantastic organic sandwiches on a cosy canal-side terrace. (p52)

Best Bakeries

Patisserie Holtkamp You're in good company here, as

the gilded royal coat of arms outside attests. (p83)

Bakhuys Amsterdam Family-run bakery making sourdough bread, pizza and pastries. (p89)

Baking Lab A communal oven, baking classes and heavenly breads. (p140)

Van Stapele Koekmakerij Melt-in-your-mouth cookies baked fresh every 10 minutes. (p52)

Eating Out Top Tips

○ Book ahead at midrange and top-end restaurants. Many places offer online bookings.

○ Lots of establishments don't accept credit cards or apply a 5% surcharge for their use. Conversely, an increasing number of places accept cards only.

Bar Open

Amsterdam's nightlife is legendary. Beyond the Red Light District, Leidseplein and Rembrandtplein, the clubbing scene has expanded thanks to 24-hour-licensed venues. Yet you can easily avoid its wilder side: Amsterdam remains a café (pub) society where the pursuit of pleasure focuses on cosiness and charm.

Cafés

Amsterdam is famed for its historic *bruin cafés* (brown cafes; traditional Dutch pubs). The name comes from their dark timber and centuries-old nicotine stains (recent aspirants slap on brown paint to catch up). Most importantly, the city's brown cafes provide an atmosphere conducive to conversation and the prized *gezelligheid* (conviviality, cosiness).

Borrel

Borrel in Dutch means, quite simply, 'drink' – as in a glass of spirits, traditionally *jenever* (Dutch gin). But in social parlance, to be invited to *borrel* means to take part in an informal gathering for drinks, conversation and fun. It usually incorporates food, especially *borrelhapjes* (bar snacks) like *borrelnootjes* (peanuts covered in a crisp, spicy outer shell), and *kroketten* (croquettes) including *bitterballen* (small, round meat croquettes) – the name comes from the tradition of serving them with bitters, namely *jenever*.

Clubbing

Amsterdam's claim to clubbing fame is the five-day electronic-music extravaganza **Amsterdam Dance Event** (amsterdam-dance-event.nl).

Epic venues with 24-hour licences, such as **Warehouse Elementenstraat** (elementenstraat.nl), in an industrial estate at Sloterdijk, occupy repurposed buildings outside the city centre to minimise noise. Along with club nights, they mount multi-genre art exhibitions, markets and other cultural offerings.

LORNET/SHUTTERSTOCK ©

Best Brown Cafes

Café De Dokter Charming family-run haven and allegedly Amsterdam's smallest pub. (p53)

De Sluyswacht Swig in the lock-keeper's quarters across from Rembrandt's house. (pictured; p158)

In 't Aepjen Candles burn all day in this time-warped, 500-year-old house. (p54)

Hoppe A legendary Amsterdam establishment. Look for lively crowds spilling onto the Spui. (p54)

Best Breweries

Brouwerij 't IJ Wonderful independent brewery at the foot of De Gooyer windmill. (p157)

Brouwerij De Prael Socially minded brewery with strong organic beers. (p53)

Brouwerij Troost Sip frothy house-made suds. (p127)

Brouwerij Poesiat & Kater Inventive brews in a waterside warehouse. (p141)

Best Cocktails

Flying Dutchmen Cocktails In a 17th-century national monument with the Netherlands' biggest backbar. (p91)

Bar Mokum Celebrates Amsterdam through streetscape decor and local spirits. (p127)

Rosalia's Menagerie Dutch-heritage-themed cocktails in vintage surrounds. (p158)

Bar Oldenhof Atmospheric 1920s-style speakeasy. (p73)

Tales & Spirits House infusions and vintage glasses. (p54)

Best Coffee

Monks Coffee Roasters Has an exceptional house blend. (p73)

Back to Black Cosy neighbourhood roastery. (p91)

Lot61 Red-hot roastery with fair-trade beans. (p112)

Scandinavian Embassy Coffee sourced from Scandinavian micro-roasteries. (p125)

Bocca Coffee One of Amsterdam's longest-running roasteries and buzzy as ever. (p92)

Treasure Hunt

During the Golden Age, Amsterdam was the world's warehouse, stuffed with riches from the far corners of the earth. The capital's cupboards are still stocked with all kinds of curios, antiques and vintage treasures, but you'll also find cutting-edge Dutch design, fashion and innovations.

Specialities & Souvenirs

Dutch fashion is all about cool, practical designs that don't get caught in bike spokes. Dutch-designed homewares bring a stylish touch to everyday objects. Antiques, art and vintage goodies also rank high on the local list. Popular gifts include tulip bulbs, Gouda cheese and bottles of *jenever* (Dutch gin). Blue-and-white Delft pottery is a widely available quality souvenir. And, of course, clogs and bicycle bells are in abundant supply.

Shopping Streets

The busiest shopping streets are Kalverstraat by the Dam, and Leidsestraat, which leads into Leidseplein. Both are lined with department stores such as Dutch retailers Hema and De Bijenkorf. In the Old South (Oud Zuid), PC Hooftstraat lines up luxury brands like Chanel, Diesel and Gucci.

Boutiques & Antiques

At the top of the Jordaan, Haarlemmerstraat and Haarlemmerdijk

Shopping Top Tips

- Department stores and large shops generally open seven days; some smaller shops close on Sunday and/or Monday.

- Many shops stay open to 9pm Thursday.

- Useful words: *kassa* (cashier), *korting* (discount) and *uitverkoop* (clearance sale).

FOOTTOO/SHUTTERSTOCK ©

have hip boutiques and food shops. Just to the south, the Negen Straatjes (Nine Streets) offer a satisfying browse among offbeat, pint-sized shops.

Antique and art buffs should head for the Southern Canal Ring's Spiegel Quarter, along Spiegelgracht and Nieuwe Spiegelstraat.

Best Markets

Albert Cuypmarkt Vibrant street market spilling over with food, fashion and bargain finds. (p123)

Noordermarkt Trawl for organic food and vintage clothes. (p77)

Waterlooplein Flea Market Piles of curios for treasure hunters. (p149)

Best Dutch Design

Frozen Fountain Furniture and homewares showcase. (p76)

X Bank Emporium/gallery with monthly changing displays. (p56)

Moooi Founded by famed Dutch designers Marcel Wanders and Casper Vissers. (p94)

DSign High-end Dutch creations. (p161)

Best Fashion

Anna + Nina Jewellery atelier from a local design brand. (p77)

Collect the Label Wearable art by local creators. (p65)

Rain Couture Fashionable wet-weather wear. (p95)

Shirt Shop Stylish patterned shirts for the guys. (p95)

Best Souvenirs

Bloemenmarkt Bulbs, bulbs and more bulbs fill Amsterdam's 'floating' flower market. (pictured; p83)

Mark Raven Grafiek Arty, beyond-the-norm T-shirts and prints of the city. (p56)

Maker Store Made by local artists. (p116)

By Popular Demand Cute gifts like Miffy tea towels. (p56)

Museums & Galleries

Amsterdam's world-class museums draw millions of visitors each year. The art takes pride of place – you can't walk a kilometre without bumping into a masterpiece. Canal-house museums are another local speciality. And the city has an assortment of unique small museums from pianolas to pipes, and emerging media art spaces.

Canal-House Museums

There are two kinds of canal-house museum: the first preserves the house as a living space, with sumptuous interiors that show how the richest locals lived once upon a time, as at Museum Van Loon (p87). The other type uses the elegant structure as a backdrop for unique collections, such as the Kattenkabinet (p83) for cat art.

All the Art

The Dutch Masters helped begin the extensive art collections around town. Painters such as Johannes Vermeer, Frans Hals and Rembrandt van Rijn worked during the Golden Age, when a new, bourgeois society of merchants and shopkeepers was spending money to brighten homes and workplaces with fresh paintings. The masters' output from that era now fills the city's top museums.

Other Treasures

The Netherlands' maritime prowess during the Golden Age also filled the galleries of local institutions. Silver, porcelain and colonial artefacts picked up on distant voyages form the basis of collections in the Rijksmuseum, Amsterdam Museum, Het Scheepvaartmuseum and Wereldmuseum Amsterdam.

Best Art Museums

Rijksmuseum The Netherlands' top treasure house bursts with Rembrandts, Vermeers, Delftware and more. (p98)

Van Gogh Museum Hangs the world's largest collection of the extraordinary artist's vivid canvases. (p102)

PIETER ROOVERS/SHUTTERSTOCK ©

Museum Rembrandthuis Immerse yourself in the old master's wonderfully preserved former studio and home. (p146)

Stedelijk Museum Renowned modern art from Picasso to Mondrian to Warhol. (pictured: p109)

H'ART Blockbuster exhibits in collaboration with major art institutions. (p86)

Foam Changing exhibits by world-renowned photographers. (p87)

Best History Museums

Anne Frank Huis The Secret Annexe and Anne's claustrophobic bedroom serve as chilling reminders of WWII. (p62)

Amsterdam Museum Follow the twists and turns of Amsterdam's convoluted history. (p87)

Verzetsmuseum Learn about WWII Dutch resistance fighters during the Nazi occupation. (p152)

Wereldmuseum Amsterdam Explores diverse global cultures through art and artefacts, offering insights into human history and traditions. (p134)

Top Tips for Culture Vultures

○ Pre-book tickets for the big museums. Many tickets have allocated time slots and must be purchased online ahead of time.

○ **I amsterdam Card** and **Museumkaart** (p179) holders still need to reserve their time slots.

○ Museums are quietest in the late afternoon and evening. Friday, Saturday and Sunday are the busiest days.

Show Time

Amsterdam supports a flourishing arts scene, with loads of big concert halls, theatres, cinemas, comedy clubs and other performance venues filled on a regular basis. Music fans are superbly catered for here, and there is a fervent subculture for just about every genre, especially jazz, classical, rock and avant-garde beats.

Music

Jazz is extremely popular, from far-out, improvisational stylings to more traditional notes. The Bimhuis (p159) is the big game in town, drawing musicians from around the globe, though its vibe is more that of a funky little club. Smaller jazz venues abound and it's easy to find a live combo.

Amsterdam's classical-music scene, with top international orchestras, conductors and soloists crowding the agenda, is the envy of many European cities. Choose between the flawless Concertgebouw (p114) or dramatic Muziekgebouw aan 't IJ (p159) for the main shows.

Many of the city's clubs also host rock bands. Huge touring names often play smallish venues such as the Melkweg (p93) and Paradiso (p93); it's a real treat to catch one of your favourites here.

Comedy & Theatre

English-language comedy thrives in Amsterdam,

Entertainment Top Tips

○ **We Are Public** (wearepublic.nl) offers members free (or heavily discounted) tickets. The one-off fee (under/over 30 years €15/20) can be worth it for multiple shows.

○ Check **I amsterdam** (iamsterdam.com) for events listings; for movie screenings visit **Film Ladder** (filmladder.nl/amsterdam).

BEN HOUDIJK/SHUTTERSTOCK ©

especially around the Jordaan. Local theatre tends towards the edgy and experimental.

Cinema

Amsterdam is cinephile heaven, with oodles of arthouse cinemas. Numerous screenings are in English.

Best Rock

Melkweg Housed in a former dairy, it's Amsterdam's coolest club-gallery-cinema-concert hall. (pictured, Hayley Kiyoko performance; p93)

Paradiso One-time church that preaches a gospel of rock. (p93)

De Nieuwe Anita Rock out by the stage behind the bookcase-concealed door. (p75)

Best Classical & Opera

Muziekgebouw aan 't IJ Stunning high-tech temple of the performing arts. (p159)

Concertgebouw World-renowned concert hall with superb acoustics. (p114)

Best Comedy & Theatre

Boom Chicago Laugh-out-loud improv-style comedy in the Jordaan. (p74)

Tobacco Theater Cabaret and theatre productions in a former tobacco auction house. (p55)

Best Cinemas

EYE Filmmuseum The Netherlands' striking film centre shows quality films of all kinds. (p167)

Koninklijk Theater Tuschinski Amsterdam's most beautiful cinema, with a sumptuous art-deco Amsterdam School interior. (p93)

Movies The city's oldest cinema dates from 1912. (p75)

Lab 111 Cult films in an ex-science lab. (p116)

Under the Radar

Throughout Amsterdam there are opportunities to discover lesser-known attractions including unusual museums and galleries, beautiful outdoor spaces and unique trips on picturesque canals. The compact size of the Dutch capital means you don't have to venture far to explore fascinating local haunts off the beaten track.

Canal Cruise Alternatives

Getting out on the water gives you a different perspective on Amsterdam's canals, with plenty of alternatives to sightseeing cruises.

Canal tours with a twist include the laid-back, irreverent outings run by **Those Dam Boat Guys** (thosedamboat guys.com). **Rederij Lampedusa** (rederij lampedusa.nl) provides a poignant insight into Amsterdam's immigration aboard a former refugee boat.

Green Escapes

The city's parks, less visited by travellers, are more than just manicured marvels – you can discover genuine local life here.

Escape the crowds, sunbathe, picnic and discover nature and wildlife. Westerpark (p79), a leafy expanse created from a former gasworks, is now home to lush lawns and wading pools.

At Sarphatipark (p123), locals enjoy pond-side picnics from De Pijp wine and cheese shops. Beautiful Oosterpark (p138), a sprawling green space in Amsterdam's east, is close to the even more bucolic Flevopark, with a magical *jenever* distillery (p141).

Further out, you can escape into the countryside in the forests of Amsterdamse Bos (p115) in the south (which can be reached by vintage tram) or Amsterdam's oldest forest, WH Vliegenbos (p168), in Amsterdam Noord.

IVO ANTONIE DE ROOIJ/SHUTTERSTOCK ©

Best Under-the-Radar Museums

Below the Surface Staggering array of archaeological finds unearthed during the construction of the north–south metro line. (p48)

Allard Pierson Museum Human history from the Nile to the Amstel over 10,000 years. (p50)

Pianola Museum A one-of-a-kind museum collection of pianolas and thousands of music rolls. (p68)

Amsterdam Pipe Museum A fascinating collection of pipes from over 60 countries in an elegant canal house. (p88)

Stadsarchief Get a revealing insight into Amsterdam's history at the city archives. (p83)

Best Under-the-Radar Galleries

Moco Museum Exceptional modern and contemporary art in a beautiful private villa. (pictured; p109)

Museum of the Mind | Outsider Art Champions artists whose work is an inner expression not influenced by artistic movements or commercialism. (p87)

Kattenkabinet Quirky feline art in a beautiful Golden Bend canal house. (p83)

Huis Marseille A photography lover's dream for its revolving door of large-scale temporary exhibitions. (p68)

NDSM Fuse Donation-based contemporary art atop the NDSM Loods. (p167)

Best Under-the-Radar Hangouts

Hannekes Boom Huge waterside beer garden and a festive local atmosphere. (p158)

OCCII A former squat giving the night to edgy alternative bands. (p107)

Vondelbunker Behind a graffitied door, a wartime shelter hosts live music and film nights run by volunteers. (p116)

Sexyland World Funky Noord haunt with roller discos and food pop-ups. (p165)

Cinetol Arts centre with established and emerging acts, art exhibitions, film screenings, markets and more. (p129)

Canals

STEVE PHOTOGRAPHY/SHUTTERSTOCK ©

Amsterdammers have always known that their Canal Ring, built during the Golden Age, is extraordinary. UNESCO made it official in 2010, when it listed the waterways as a World Heritage Site. Today the city has 165 canals spanned by 1753 bridges. The best views of all are from out on the water.

Best Views

Golden Bend Where Golden Age magnates built their mansions along the regal Herengracht. (p83)

Reguliersgracht The 'canal of seven bridges' is one of Amsterdam's most photographed vistas. (p89)

Prinsengracht The liveliest of Amsterdam's inner canals, with restaurants, shops and houseboats lining the quays. (pictured; p70)

Brouwersgracht Amsterdammers say this is the most beautiful canal. (p70)

Best Canal-Related Museums

Grachtenmuseum Amsterdam Inventive multimedia displays explain how the Canal Ring and its houses were built. (p68)

Houseboat Museum Discover how *gezellig* (cosy) houseboat living can be aboard this 1914 barge-turned-museum. (p70)

Best Canal-Side Hangs

De Belhamel At the head of the Herengracht, this superb restaurant has tables along the canal. (p71)

Buffet van Odette Simple, creative cooking overlooking the Prinsengracht's crooked canal houses. (p88)

't Smalle Dock your boat right by the stone terrace of the 18th-century former *jenever* distillery. (p73)

Canal Life Top Tips

○ Virtually none of Amsterdam's canals have fences or barriers. Keep a close eye on young children.

○ When canals freeze, only ice skate if you see large groups of people. Be very careful at the edges and under bridges, as these are areas with weak ice.

Cycling

Bicycles are more common than cars in Amsterdam, and to roll like a local you'll need a two-wheeler. Rent one from the myriad outlets around town or from your accommodation, and the whole city becomes your playground. Cycling is the quintessential activity while you visit.

KAVALENKAU/SHUTTERSTOCK ©

Journey Planning

The official route planner of the Dutch Cyclists' Union is **Fietsersbond** (routeplanner.fietsersbond.nl). **Route You** (routeyou.com) is good for planning out scenic routes. For up-to-date info on things such as bicycle-repair shops, check out **Holland Cycling** (holland-cycling.com).

Road Rules & Cycling Tips

Helmets aren't compulsory but are recommended; most bike-hire places rent them out.

Amsterdam has over 500km of bike paths. Use the bicycle lane on the road's right-hand side, marked by white lines and bike symbols. Cycling on footpaths is illegal.

Cycle in the same direction as traffic and adhere to all traffic lights and signs. Hand signal when turning.

A bell is mandatory. After dark, a white or yellow headlight and red tail light are required by law.

Cross tram rails at a sharp angle to avoid getting stuck.

Park (and lock up!) your bike only in designated bicycle racks or risk its removal by the police.

If your bike goes missing, call the **Fietsdepot** (Bike Depository) on 020-334 45 22 to see if it was removed by the city. If not, call the police on 0900 88 44 to report it stolen.

Best Cycling Spots

Vondelpark Urban oasis. (pictured; p106)

Eastern Islands Contemporary architecture.

Amsterdam Noord Windmills and farmland.

For Free

Although the costs of Amsterdam's accommodation and dining can mount up, there is a bright side. Not only is the entire Canal Ring a UNESCO World Heritage Site (effectively a free living museum), but there are plenty of things to do and see that are free (or virtually free).

WOLF-PHOTOGRAPHY/SHUTTERSTOCK ©

Best Free Sights

Rijksmuseum Gardens The Renaissance and Baroque gardens, with roses, hedges and statues, are free (including occasional sculpture exhibitions). (p98)

Begijnhof Explore the 14th-century hidden courtyard and its clandestine churches. (p48)

Stadsarchief You never know what treasures you'll find in the vaults of the city's archives. (p83)

Albert Cuypmarkt Amsterdam's busiest market; the city's many bazaars are free to browse. (p123)

NDSM Loods Wander through these vast artist studios in Amsterdam Noord. (p167)

NEMO Science Museum roof terrace One of the best views of Amsterdam extends from the roof of this landmark building. (p152)

Best Free Entertainment

Concertgebouw Sharpen your elbows for Wednesday's lunchtime concert (September to June), often a rehearsal for the evening performance. (p114)

Bimhuis Jazz sessions hot up the revered venue on Tuesday nights. (p159)

Openluchttheater Vondelpark's outdoor theatre puts on concerts and kids' shows in summer. (pictured; p107)

Oosterpark Summer tango sessions. (p138)

King's Day The ultimate party, this is one of many festivals and events that are free. (p130)

Top Tips For Freebies

○ Students and seniors should bring ID and flash it at every opportunity for reduced admission fees.

○ Download the Dutch app 'Publicroam' for free wi-fi hot spots around the city.

Tours

Guided tours are a great way to get to grips with the city, especially if you're short on time. Walking tours abound, including themed tours covering subjects such as history, architecture or food. Cycling tours and boat tours are also ubiquitous.

ANDREW BALCOMBE/SHUTTERSTOCK ©

Best Walking

Hungry Birds Street Food Tours (hungrybirds. nl) Guides take you 'off the eaten track' to chow on Dutch and ethnic specialities. Lasting around five hours, tours visit local hot spots from street vendors to family-run premises.

Mee in Mokum (gildeamsterdam.nl) Low-priced two- to three-hour walkabouts, led by volunteers. Reserve at least two business days ahead.

Arcam Architectural Tours (Stichting Architectuurcentrum Amsterdam; arcam.nl) Architecture buffs can sign up for guided walking (and cycling) tours of the city run by the Amsterdam Architecture Foundation.

Best Cycling

Mike's Bike Tours (mikesbiketoursamsterdam. com) City and country tours.

Yellow Bike (yellowbike. nl) Year-round city tours and summer Waterland tours.

Best Boat

Rederji Lampedusa (rederijlampedusa.nl) Tours aboard former refugee boats, with commentary on the history of immigration.

Blue Boat Company (pictured; blueboat.nl) Main tours glide by the top sights. It also runs nighttime trips, children's pirate-themed cruises and drag-queen bingo cruises.

Plastic Whale (plasticwhale.com) Fish waste from Amsterdam's waterways with nets made from retrieved and recycled plastic waste

Kayak in Amsterdam (kayakinamsterdam.com) Guided tours of key canal sights: one-hour intro tours, two-hour classic canal tours or three-hour explorer tours.

Best Tram

Electrische Museumtramlijn Amsterdam (Tram Museum Amsterdam; museumtramlijn.org) Vintage tram trips to Amsterdamse Bos and city sightseeing: line 20 departs from Dam on the first and third Saturdays of the month and Sundays on a two-hour circular route, passing the Westerkerk, Rijksmuseum and Rembrandtplein.

For Kids

Breathe easy: you've landed in one of Europe's most kid-friendly cities. The famous Dutch tolerance extends to children and Amsterdammers cheerfully accommodate them. You'll find that virtually all quarters of the city – except the Red Light District, of course – are fair game for the younger set.

DUTCHMEN PHOTOGRAPHY/SHUTTERSTOCK ©

Best Activities for Kids

NEMO Science Museum Kid-focused, hands-on science labs inside and a terrace with a splashy summer water feature. (p152)

Het Scheepvaartmuseum Climb aboard the full-scale, 17th-century replica ship and check out the cannons. (p152)

Wereldmuseum Amsterdam Learn to yodel, sit in a yurt or travel via otherworldly exhibits. (p134)

Vondelpark Space-age slides at the western end, playground in the middle, duck ponds throughout. (p106)

Artis Zoo Extrovert monkeys, big cats, shimmying fish and a planetarium provide thrills. (pictured; p153)

OBA: Centrale Bibliotheek Amsterdam Has a whole children's floor with story times, reading lounges and English books. (p154)

Micropia The world's first microbe museum has a wall of poop, a kissing meter and other inventive exhibits. (p153)

Wondr Bouncy castles and ball pits galore in an interactive art centre–play space. (p168)

Top Tips For Families

○ At many tourist sites, the cut-off age for free or reduced-rate entry is 12. Some sights only provide free entry to children under six.

○ Most bike-rental shops hire bikes with baby or child seats.

○ Many higher-end hotels arrange babysitting services for a fee.

Best Kids' Shops

Het Oud-Hollandsch Snoepwinkeltje Stocks jar after jar of Dutch penny sweets. (p72)

Mechanisch Speelgoed Nostalgic wind-up toys. (p77)

Donsje Adorable kids' clothes. (p117)

LGBTIQ+

To call Amsterdam a queer capital doesn't express just how welcoming and open the scene is here. The Netherlands was the first country to legalise same-sex marriage (in 2001), so it's no surprise that Amsterdam's gay scene is among the world's largest.

DUTCHMEN PHOTOGRAPHY/SHUTTERSTOCK ©

Party Zones

Warmoesstraat in the Red Light District hosts the infamous, kink-filled leather and fetish bars. Nearby, at the upper end of the **Zeedijk**, crowds spill onto laid-back bar terraces. The area around **Rembrandtplein** (aka the 'Amstel area') has traditional pubs and brown cafes, some with a campy bent. Leidseplein has a smattering of high-action clubs along **Kerkstraat**. The trendy hot spots of **Reguliersdwarsstraat** draw the beautiful crowd.

Best LGBTIQ+ Hangouts

't Mandje Amsterdam's oldest gay bar is a trinket-covered beauty. (p54)

Montmartre Legendary bar where Dutch ballads and old top-40 hits tear the roof off. (p92)

Blend XL Buzzing street terrace and dance floor with a disco ball. (p92)

Taboo Bar Drag shows and party games. (p92)

LGBTIQ+ Top Tips

○ **Gay Amsterdam** (gayamsterdam.com) lists hotels, shops and clubs, and provides maps.

○ Information kiosk and souvenir shop **Pink Point** (pinkpoint.nl) has details of parties, events and social groups.

○ **Pride Amsterdam** (pride.amsterdam/en; ⏰ late Jul–early Aug) features the world's only waterborne Pride parade (pictured).

○ Join a two-hour walking tour of Amsterdam's LGBTIQ+ history spanning 400 years (specialamsterdamtours.nl).

Responsible Travel

Prompted by the climate crisis and the local impact of overtourism, Amsterdam is rapidly emerging as one of Europe's most sustainable cities. The Netherlands is aiming for a waste-free circular economy by 2050, using reusable and renewable raw materials. Inspired initiatives citywide mean visitors can also play a part.

Smart Mobility

Cycling The traditional, emissions-free way to roll in Amsterdam.

Canal Bike Jump aboard a pedal boat from this outfitter. (p71)

Boaty Electric boats you can drive yourself. (p123)

Activities

Plastic Whale Help clean Amsterdam's waterways. (p27)

Tours That Matter (toursthatmatter.com) Offers tours centring Amsterdam in the context of Dutch colonialism and gentrification.

Rederij Lampedusa Hear personal stories aboard these cruises on former refugee boats. (p22)

Fashion for Good World-first sustainable-fashion museum, highlighting alarming stats such as 60% of all clothing goes to landfill or is burned. (p49)

Climate Change & Travel

It's impossible to ignore the impact we have when travelling, and the importance of making changes where we can.

Lonely Planet urges all travellers to engage with their travel carbon footprint. There are many carbon calculators online to estimate the carbon emissions generated by a journey; try resurgence.org. Many airlines and booking sites offer an option to offset the impact of greenhouse gas emissions by supporting climate-friendly initiatives around the world.

We continue to offset the carbon footprint of all Lonely Planet staff travel, while recognising this is a mitigation more than a solution.

RESTAURANT DE KAS

PROCREATORS/SHUTTERSTOCK ©

Circular Fashion

Mercer Local designer that makes sneakers from pineapple leather. (p130)

Property Of... Backpacks and tote bags from recycled plastic that imitates canvas. (p95)

Grice Inspired styles incorporate zero-waste techniques and recycled and upcycled fabrics. (p131)

Zipper Vintage shop till you drop. (p65)

Eco-Buys

Marie-Stella-Maris Proceeds from cosmetics go towards clean-water initiatives. (p76)

Het Faire Oosten Stocked with sustainable creations such as raincoats from recycled bottles. (p143)

Donsje Donates proceeds to a children's charity. (p117)

Van Dijk & Ko Wonderful antiques seeking new homes. (p165)

Sustainable Dining

De Ceuvel An innovative sustainability 'playground' reviving a once-polluted harbour with a building made from recycled materials and a delicious zero-waste menu. (p170)

Mediamatic ETEN The bar/restaurant at art, design and life-sciences hub Mediamatic uses produce from its dockside greenhouses. (p157)

Gartine Slow-food sandwiches featuring produce grown in the cafe's garden. (p51)

De Kas Grows its organic produce on site. (pictured; p138)

Jacob's Juice Fresh-squeezed juices from otherwise-discarded fruit and vegetables. (p128)

Green Sleeping

Conscious Hotel The chain for those seeking a greener sleep.

Cocomama This hostel offers an environmentally conscious option for those on a budget.

Resources

City of Amsterdam (amsterdam.nl) Amsterdam's strategy for becoming fully circular.

Government of the Netherlands (government.nl) National sustainability goals.

Four Perfect Days

Day 1

IVICA DRUSANY/SHUTTERSTOCK ©

Begin by viewing the masterpieces at Museumplein's **Rijksmuseum** (p98) and **Van Gogh Museum** (p102). Modern-art buffs might want to swap one for the **Stedelijk Museum** (p109).

Explore the secret courtyard and gardens at the **Begijnhof** (p48) in the Medieval Centre. Stroll to the **Dam** (p49), where the **Royal Palace** (Koninklijk Paleis; p42) and **Nieuwe Kerk** (pictured; p48) provide a dose of Dutch history. In the Red Light District, the **Oude Kerk** (p44) has historical and art exhibitions.

Sip *jenever* (Dutch gin) standing up like a local at **Wynand Fockink** (p43), and settle into a *bruin café* (traditional Dutch pub), such as **In 't Aepjen** (p54).

Day 2

ANTON_IVANOV/SHUTTERSTOCK ©

After brunch in De Pijp at a local hangout like **Coffee & Coconuts** (p125), browse Amsterdam's largest street market, the **Albert Cuypmarkt** (p123). Then get shaken up, heated up and 'bottled' like a beer at the **Heineken Experience** (pictured; p123).

Cross into the Southern Canal Ring to check out the opulent canal-house lifestyle at **Museum Van Loon** (p87), feline art at the **Kattenkabinet** (p83) and bulbs galore at the **Bloemenmarkt** (p83).

After dark, par-tee at hyperactive, neon-lit **Leidseplein** (p87), surrounded by good-time clubs and *bruin cafés*. **Paradiso** (p93) and **Melkweg** (p93) host the coolest agendas.

Day 3

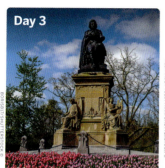

BORISB17/SHUTTERSTOCK ©

Take a spin around Amsterdam's beloved **Vondelpark** (pictured; p106). It's easy to explore on a morning jaunt – and all the better if you have a bicycle to zip by the ponds, gardens and sculptures.

Immerse yourself in the Western Canal Ring's **Negen Straatjes** (p75), a noughts-and-crosses board of speciality shops. At the nearby **Anne Frank Huis** (p62), the claustrophobic rooms give an all-too-real feel for Anne's life in hiding, as does seeing her diary.

Spend the evening in the Jordaan, the chummy district embodying the Amsterdam of yore. Hoist a glass on a canal-side terrace at **'t Smalle** (p73) or quaff beers at heaps of other *gezellig* (cosy) haunts.

Day 4

ALEXANDER TOLSTYKH/SHUTTERSTOCK ©

Mosey through **Waterlooplein Flea Market** (pictured; p149) in Nieuwmarkt before visiting Rembrandt's studio at the **Museum Rembrandthuis** (p146). Discover Resistance history at the **Verzetsmuseum** (p152), or sea treasures at **Het Scheepvaartmuseum** (p152).

Cross the the IJ River to up-and-coming Amsterdam Noord. Catch cinematic exhibits at the **EYE Filmmuseum** (p167) and contemporary-art exhibitions at the **NDSM Loods** (p167) or **Straat** (p167). Ascend **A'DAM Tower** (p167) for panoramic views.

Back on the city side of the IJ, enjoy a drink at **De Ysbreeker** (p59), overlooking the Amstel river.

Need to Know

For detailed information, see Survival Guide (p172)

Currency
Euro (€)

Language
Dutch; English widely spoken

Visas
Generally not required for stays up to 90 days; from mid-2025, non-EU nationals will need to apply for ETIAS pre-authorisation online.

Money
ATMs widely available. Some establishments accept only cash, or only cards.

Mobile Phones
Ask your home provider about an international plan. Alternatively, local prepaid SIM cards are widely available.

Time
Central European Time (GMT/UTC plus one hour)

Tipping
Tip 5% to 10% for cafe snacks, 10% for a restaurant meal, 5% to 10% in a taxi.

Daily Budget

Budget: Less than €150
Dorm bed: €25–60
Supermarkets and lunchtime specials for food: €20
Boom Chicago late-night show ticket: €20
Bike hire per day: €16

Midrange: €150–300
Double room: from €150
Three-course dinner in casual restaurant: €40
Concertgebouw ticket: €50
Canal cruise: €20

Top end: More than €300
Four-star hotel double room: from €250
Five-course dinner in top restaurant: from €80
Private canal-boat rental for 90 minutes: from €90

Advance Planning

Four months before Book your accommodation, especially if you're visiting in summer or on a weekend.

Two months before Check club and performing-arts calendars and buy tickets for anything that looks appealing.

Two weeks before Make dinner reservations at your must-eat restaurants, reserve walking or cycling tours, and purchase tickets online to popular attractions like the Van Gogh Museum, Anne Frank Huis and Rijksmuseum.

Arriving in Amsterdam

✈ From Schiphol International Airport

Trains to Centraal Station depart every 10 minutes or so from 6am to 12.30am, hourly at other times; the 15-minute trip costs €5.90. Taxis cost €50.

🚃 From Centraal Station

The main train station is in central Amsterdam with many tram and metro lines connecting it to the rest of the city; taxis queue near the front entrance (towards the west side).

🚃 From Bus Stations

International coach company FlixBus uses several stops in and around Amsterdam; check your ticket for information.

Getting Around

GVB passes in chip-card form (€7.50) are the most convenient option for public transport.

🚶 Walking

Central Amsterdam is easily covered on foot.

🚲 Bicycle

Rental companies are everywhere; bikes cost about €16 daily.

🚃 Tram

Frequent and ubiquitous, operating between 6am and 12.30am.

🚃 Bus & Metro

Primarily serve outer districts; metro 52 links Amsterdam Noord with the World Trade Centre in the south via the city centre and De Pijp.

⚓ Ferry

Free ferries to Amsterdam Noord depart from docks behind Centraal Station.

Amsterdam Neighbourhoods

Medieval Centre & Red Light District (p41)

Amsterdam's medieval core mixes fairy-tale Golden Age buildings, *bruin cafés* and the lurid Red Light District.

Western Canal Ring & the Jordaan (p61)

The Jordaan teems with cosy pubs and lanes ideal for getting lost. The Western Canal Ring unfurls quirky boutiques and waterside cafés.

Anne Frank Huis

Koninklijk Paleis

Vondelpark

Rijksmuseum

Van Gogh Museum

Vondelpark & the South (p97)

Vondelpark is a green lung with personality, adjacent to the genteel South, home to Amsterdam's grandest museums.

Southern Canal Ring (p81)

By day, visit the city's less-heralded museums. By night, party at the clubs around Leidseplein and Rembrandtplein.

Amsterdam Noord (p163)
Once industrial, Amsterdam's north is now home to some of the city's most cutting-edge creative venues.

Oude Kerk

Museum Rembrandthuis

Wereldmuseum Amsterdam

Nieuwmarkt, Plantage & the Eastern Islands (p145)
See Rembrandt's studio and Amsterdam's Jewish heritage in Nieuwmarkt, and gardens and a beery windmill in the Plantage.

De Pijp (p119)
Ethnic meets trendy in this recently gentrified neighbourhood, best sampled at the colourful Albert Cuypmarkt and multicultural eateries that surround it.

Oosterpark & East of the Amstel (p133)
One of the city's most culturally diverse areas, with Moroccan and Turkish enclaves and some great bars and restaurants.

Explore
Amsterdam

Amsterdam Tours

Leidseplein (p87) WOLF-PHOTOGRAPHY/SHUTTERSTOCK ©

Explore ◈
Medieval Centre & Red Light District

Amsterdam's oldest quarter is remarkably preserved, recalling its Golden Age heyday. The Amstel's original river-mouth, Damrak, stretches south to the Royal Palace on the Dam. East, around shopping hub Kalverstraat, side streets brim with 17th-century jenever (gin) tasting rooms, cosy bruin cafés (pubs), boutiques and atmospheric restaurants. West are the narrow alleyways of the Red Light District (aka De Wallen).

The Short List

◦ **Oude Kerk (p44)** *Admiring Amsterdam's oldest surviving building, dating back to 1306.*

◦ **Koninklijk Paleis (p42)** *Marvelling at the chandeliered opulence of the city's landmark Royal Palace.*

◦ **Vleminckx (p50)** *Biting into crisp golden fries, slathered in mayonnaise, curry or peanut sauce from Amsterdam's best frites stand.*

◦ **Wynand Fockink (p43)** *Bowling up to this 17th-century tasting house to knock back a jenever.*

Getting There & Around

🚊 Many of the city's 15 tram lines go through the neighbourhood en route to Centraal Station.

Ⓜ The Metro travels from Centraal to Amsterdam's outer neighbourhoods, and to Amsterdam Noord and Station Zuid via Rokin in the Medieval Centre.

⛴ Free ferries to Amsterdam Noord depart from the piers behind Centraal Station.

Neighbourhood Map on p46

Dam (p49) JEFF WHYTE/SHUTTERSTOCK ©

Top Experience

Marvel at the opulence of the Koninklijk Paleis

The Royal Palace began life as a town hall and was completed in 1665. Its architect, Jacob van Campen, spared no expense to display Amsterdam's wealth in a way that rivalled the grandest European buildings of the day. The result is opulence on a big scale. It's worth seeing the exterior at night, when the palace is dramatically floodlit.

◎ MAP P46, B5

Royal Palace

paleisamsterdam.nl

A King's Residence

Officially, the Dutch king, Willem-Alexander, lives in this landmark palace and pays a symbolic rent, though his actual residence is in Den Haag. If he's not here in Amsterdam, visitors have the opportunity to come in and wander around the monumental building.

The 1st Floor

Most of the rooms are spread over the 1st floor, which is awash in chandeliers (51 in total), along with damasks, gilded clocks and some spectacular paintings by artists including Ferdinand Bol and Jacob de Wit. The great *burgerzaal* (citizens' hall) that occupies the heart of the building was envisioned as a schematic of the world, with Amsterdam as its centre. Check out the maps inlaid in the floor; they show the eastern and western hemispheres, with a 1654 celestial map in the middle.

Empire-Style Decor

In 1808 the building became the palace of King Louis, Napoleon Bonaparte's brother. In a classic slip-up in the new lingo, French-born Louis told his subjects here that he was the 'rabbit' (*konijn*) of Holland, when he actually meant 'king' (*koning,* which had the old spelling variation *konink*). Napoleon dismissed him two years later. Louis left behind about 1000 pieces of Empire-style furniture and decorative artworks. As a result, the palace now holds one of the world's largest collections from the period.

★ Top Tips

○ The Royal Palace is still used for state functions and often closes for such events, especially during April, May, November and December. The schedule is posted on the website's calendar.

○ When you enter, be sure to pick up the free audioguide, which vividly details the palace's main features.

✕ Take a Break

Try the famed Dutch herring at **Rob Wigboldus Vishandel** (☎020-626 33 88), a teeny fish shop with excellent sandwiches.

Sip *jenever* (Dutch gin) from a tulip-shaped glass at the **Wynand Fockink** (wynand-fockink.nl) tasting room, dating back to 1679.

Top Experience

Visit Amsterdam's oldest building, the Oude Kerk

A historical and cultural treasure, Amsterdam's Oude Kerk dates back to 1306. Originally Catholic and now Protestant, the Gothic-style structure holds the city's oldest church bell, a stunning Vater-Müller organ and 15th-century choir stalls. The church was built to honour the city's patron saint, St Nicholas.

MAP P46, D4

Old Church
oudekerk.nl

History

Originally, this site was home to a graveyard built on a mound next to the Amstel river and wooden chapel constructed around 1213. A stone church replaced it in 1306 and it was consecrated in 1309 as the Catholic St Nicolaaskerk. It became known as the Oude Kerk (Old Church) once the Nieuwe Kerk was built in 1409. The Oude Kerk's north and south transepts were added in the 15th century, and the Lady Chapel was completed in 1552. After Amsterdam's Catholic city council was deposed in 1578, the ransacked Oude Kerk went on to become a Protestant place of worship as part of the Dutch Reformed Church. Exhibits trace its long history.

Famous Graves

Many famous Amsterdammers are buried under the worn tombstones set in the floor, including Rembrandt's wife, Saskia van Uylenburgh. Each year on 9 March at 8.39am, a beam of light touches her grave. Other notable graves are those of diamond dealer Kiliaen van Rensselaer, naval hero Jacob van Heemskerck, organist Jan Pieterszoon Sweelinck and the family tomb of statesman Cornelis de Graeff. Some 60,000 citizens lie beneath the church.

Visiting the Oude Kerk

Standout historical features include Amsterdam's oldest church bell (1450), 15th-century choir stalls with graphic misericords (wooden carvings) and Europe's largest medieval wooden vaulted ceiling. The tower rises 67m (check if guided tours are available).

Contemporary art exhibitions are a highlight. During concerts, you can hear the magnificent Vater-Müller organ (first built in 1726; rebuilt in 1742), 1965 transept organ, Italian organ and cabinet organ.

★ Top Tips

o Buy tickets in advance online or at the entrance.

o Admission covers entry to the historical exhibits in the side rooms as well as the current contemporary art exhibition in the church hall.

o The free audioguide details the church's history and highlights.

o The church may close during the changeover of art exhibitions or when preparing for concerts.

✗ Take a Break

Attached to the church, **Koffieschenkerij** (koffieschenkerij.com), serving hot and cold drinks and lovely cakes, has a sunny garden blooming with tulips in spring.

Nearby, **Ivy & Bros** (facebook.com/ivyandbros) is great for all-day brunches, coffee and art (most of its artworks, furniture and crockery are for sale).

For reviews see

Top Experiences	p42
Sights	p48
Eating	p50
Drinking	p53
Entertainment	p55
Shopping	p56

200 m
0.1 miles

De Ruijterkade

Prins Hendrikkade

Centraal Station

Centraal Station (east side)

Centraal Station (west side)

Centraal Station

Centraal Station

Open Havenfront

Prins Hendrikkade

Nicolaasbasiliek 10

Prins Hendrikkade

Oudezijds Kolk

28

Geldersekade

Gelderskade

Binnen Bantammerstr

Nam Kee New King

Zeedijk

Stormst

27

Dutch Courage 25

Zeedijk

Amstl

Oudezijds Voorburgwal

He Hua Temple

Korte Niezel

St Antonbr

Voorburgwal

Museum Ons' Lieve Heer op Solder 3

21

Warmoesstr

Oude Kerk

Proeflokaal de Ooievaar

Nieuwbrugst

Oudebrugst

Oudebrugsteeg

Warmoesstr

St Antniestr

39

Damrak

Damrak

Beurssstr

16

Haringpakkerssteeg

Martelaarsg

Paleisstr

23

Nieuwendijk

Nieuwendijk

Kolkst

St Jacobsstr

2 11 12 13 17

Onze Lieve Vrouwest

Beursplein

Nieuwezijds Kolk

Amsterdam Oersoep

18 4

Brouwersgr

Haarlemmerstr

Singel

Singel

Stromarkt

13

Kogeest

30

Oude Nieuwstr

Spuist

Nieuwezijds Voorburgwal

D van Hasseltsst

Nieuwe Nieuwstr

Nieuwe Nieuwstr

St Nicolaasstr

De Drie Fleschjes

Gravenstr

Nieuwe Kerk 1

Langestr

Korsjespoortst

26

Nieuwezijds Voorburgwal

Lijnbaansst

Blauwburgwal

Herengr

Herengr

Herenstr

Keizersgr

Keizersgr

Torenstr

Molst

Oude Leliestr

Bergstr

Herengracht

JORDAAN

35

42

40

N

NIEUWMARKT

Lastageweg
Koningsstr
Keizersstr
Dijkstr
Nieuwmarkt
Nieuwe Hoogstr
Bloedstr
Barndest
Koestr
St Antoniesbreestr
Jodenbreestr
Waterlooplein
Oude Schans
Stopera

Zwanenburgwal
Zwanenburgwal
Ververstr
Raamg
Staalstr
Nieuwe Doelenstr

Binnen Amstel
Amstel

Kloveniersburgwal
Kloveniersburgwal
Zandstr
Zandtwarstr
Groenburgwal

Oudezijds Achterburgwal
Cannabis College
38
Rusland
Slijkstr
Oudemanhuispoort
Book Market
Allard Pierson Museum
Binnengasthuis
UvA
Oude Turfmarkt

Oudezijds Voorburgwal
St Jansstr
Pijlst
Damstr
Pieter Jacobszstr
St Pietershalst
29
32
Nes
31
15
Grimburgwal
8

Warmoesstr
41
5 Below the Surface
Rokin

Dam **6**
Damrak
Kalverstr
Wijde Kapelst
Begijnenst
7
Taks
14
A'14 **Rokin**
Het Muizenhuis
9
20
17
Singel

Koninklijk Paleis
Jonge Roelenstr
St Luciensteeg
34
Nieuwezijds Voorburgwal
Gedempte Begijnensloot
Art
22
2 Amsterdam
Spui
Voetboogstr
12
Handboogstr

Paleisstr
37
33
Singel
Singel
Raadhuisstr
Spuistr
36
Raamsteeg
Oude Spiegelstr
Wijde Heist
Heist
24
11
19
Singel
Singel

Herengracht
Herengr
Herengr

Sights

Nieuwe Kerk
CHURCH

1 ◎ **MAP P46, B4**

Consecrated in 1409, this late-Gothic church is only 'new' in relation to the Oude Kerk – the city's Old Church, built a century earlier. A few monumental items dominate the spartan interior – a magnificent carved oak chancel, a bronze choir screen, a 1645-installed pipe organ and enormous stained-glass windows. It's the site of royal investitures and weddings; the building is otherwise used for exhibitions and concerts. The annual photojournalism and documentary exhibition *World Press Photo* takes place here. (New Church; nieuwekerk.nl)

Begijnhof
COURTYARD

2 ◎ **MAP P46, B7**

Dating from the early 14th century, this enclosed former convent is a peaceful haven, with tiny houses and postage-stamp gardens around a well-kept courtyard off Gedempte Begijnensloot. Within the *hof* (courtyard) is the charming 1671 **Begijnhof Kapel** (begijnhof kapelamsterdam.nl), and the **Engelse Kerk** (erc.amsterdam), built around 1392. The **Houten Huis**, the Netherlands' oldest preserved wooden house, dates from around 1465. As the courtyard is still a place of residence, visitors must be respectful (no eating, drinking, smoking, photography of houses or excessive noise).

Museum Ons' Lieve Heer op Solder
MUSEUM

3 ◎ **MAP P46, E3**

Within what looks like an ordinary canal house is an entire Catholic church. Ons' Lieve Heer op Solder (Our Dear Lord in the Attic) was built in the mid-1600s in defiance of the Calvinists. Inside you'll see labyrinthine staircases, rich artworks, period decor and the soaring, two-storey church itself. (opsolder.nl)

Amsterdam Oersoep
PUBLIC ART

4 ◎ **MAP P46, C4**

Beautiful 19th-century shopping arcade De Beurspassage was transformed in 2016 into an immersive artwork by artists Arno Coenen, Iris Roskam and Hans van Bentem. Titled *Amsterdam Oersoep* (Amsterdam Primordial Soup, as the city's canal water is known), it illustrates how water formed life in Amsterdam. Chandeliers crafted from bicycle parts illuminate its glass-mosaic-tiled ceiling; stained-glass lamps adorn its walls, where a shimmering fish fountain dispenses 'tolerance elixir' (water); and tiles depict ship wheels and anchors.

Below the Surface
GALLERY

5 ◎ **MAP P46, C6**

During the construction of Amsterdam's 2018-opened Noord/Zuidlijn (north–south metro line), more than 134,000 archaeological finds were unearthed from beneath the streets and waterways. Now 9500 of them, dating as far back as

2400 BCE, are displayed in glass cases between Rokin metro station's escalators (visitors need a valid public-transport ticket). Transport, craft and industry, buildings and interiors feature at the southern entrance. Objects at the northern entrance span science, communications, weapons, armour, recreation, personal items and clothing. (belowthesurface. amsterdam)

Dam   SQUARE

6 MAP P46, C5

This square is the very spot where Amsterdam was founded around 1270. Today, pigeons, tourists, buskers and the occasional funfair (complete with Ferris wheel) take over the grounds. It's still a national gathering spot, and if there's a major speech or demonstration, it's held here.

Fashion for Good   MUSEUM

7 MAP P46, B7

The world's first sustainable fashion museum delves into the history of fashion, the latest industry technology and innovation, and the stories behind day-to-day clothing, such as the T-shirt. The colourful and interactive exhibition may make you think twice about your own consumer behaviour, highlighting, for example, that garments travel an average of 14,000km and are handled by 100 people before you buy them. Visitors leave with a personalised 'sustainable fashion action plan', encouraging you to make environmentally conscious fashion choices. (fashionforgood.com)

Dam

LORNET/SHUTTERSTOCK ©

Medieval Centre & Red Light District Sights

Allard Pierson Museum
MUSEUM

8 ⊙ MAP P46, C7

Run by the University of Amsterdam and named for its first professor of archaeology, Allard Pierson (1831–96), this museum contains a rich archaeological collection. You'll find an actual mummy, vases from ancient Greece and Mesopotamia, a very cool wagon from the royal tombs at Salamis (Cyprus) and galleries full of other items. With an extensive range of maps, atlases and nautical charts, its cartography collection is one of the world's largest. (allardpierson.nl)

Het Muizenhuis
MUSEUM

9 ⊙ MAP P46, C8

This enchanting world in miniature is the brainchild of artist/author Karina Schaapman, who crafted a 100-room home for adorable felt mice Sam, Julia and friends, then produced a series of children's books (17 to date) on their adventures. You can see the original mansion and sets for later books (even a mouse roller-coaster) at this two-floor 'mini museum' and buy toys, books and materials to build your own mouse mansion. (themousemansion.com)

Nicolaasbasiliek
BASILICA

10 ⊙ MAP P46, F2

In plain view from Centraal Station, the magnificent cupola and neo-Renaissance towers belong to the city's first Catholic church built after Catholic worship became legal again in the 19th century. As St Nicholas is the patron saint of seafarers, it was an important symbol for Amsterdam, and elevated to a basilica minor in 2012. Interior highlights include its high altar, theatrical crown of Emperor Maximilian I and Jan Dunselman's depictions of the Stations of the Cross. (Basiliek van de Heilige Nicolaas; nicolaas-parochie.nl)

Eating

D'Vijff Vlieghen
DUTCH €€€

11 ✕ MAP P46, A7

Spread across five 17th-century canal houses, the 'Five Flies' is a jewel. Old-wood dining rooms overflow with character, featuring Delft Blue tiles and original works by Rembrandt; chairs have copper plates inscribed with the names of famous guests (Walt Disney, Mick Jagger...). Exquisite dishes may range from smoked goose breast with apple to roast veal with turnips and Dutch-crab mayonnaise. (vijffvlieghen.nl)

Vleminckx
FAST FOOD €

12 ✕ MAP P46, B8

Frying up *frites* (fries) since 1887, Amsterdam's best *friterie* has been based at this hole-in-the-wall near the Spui since 1957. The standard order of perfectly cooked crispy, fluffy *frites* is smothered in mayonnaise, though its 28 sauces also include apple, green pepper, satay and sambal. Queues often stretch down the block, but they move fast. (vleminckxdesausmeester.nl)

Red Light District Clean-Up

Amsterdam's Red Light District dates back to the 1300s, when women carrying red lanterns greeted sailors near the port. Its sex-worker windows, strip clubs, fetish shops, 'smart shops' (selling natural hallucinogens), coffeeshops (cannabis-smoking cafes) and copious bars, especially on and around Oudezijds Voorburgwal and Oudezijds Achterburgwal, have made it a magnet for hedonistic (and simply curious) visitors.

Authorities have long sought to banish boisterous revellers and crime, and reclaim its small streets and canals for residents. A clean-up agenda set out in 2007 has gathered pace post-pandemic. Having reduced the number of brothel windows, the city is endeavouring to re-locate sex workers to a purpose-built, multistorey 'erotic centre' outside the central city (at the time of writing, no location had been finalised).

To date, guided tours past sex-worker windows have been outlawed, as has smoking cannabis in central Amsterdam's streets (banning tourists from coffeeshops remains under discussion; nonprofit centre **Cannabis College** (Map p46, D5; cannabiscollege.com) has information and advice). There's now a 2am closing time for bars and clubs (3am for brothels), and a targeted 'stay away' campaign to discourage *feest-beest* ('party animals').

Ultimately, the intention is for artists and independent businesses to move in, and the expansion of cultural events such as mid-June's **Red Light Jazz Festival** (redlightjazz.com), highlighting the longstanding jazz traditions of the district.

De Silveren Spiegel DUTCH €€€

13 MAP P46, C2

Hung with replicas of Old Masters, the 'Silver Mirror' is an exceedingly elegant space inside a 1614-built, step-gabled red-brick townhouse. Delicious food served on hand-crafted porcelain might include lobster stuffed with North Sea crab with vintage Gouda foam, or Texel lamb crown with asparagus mousse and cinnamon jus. Book ahead and dress for the occasion. (desilverenspiegel.com)

Gartine   CAFE €

14 MAP P46, B7

Gartine is magical, from its covert location in an alley off Kalver-straat to its mismatched antique tableware and produce grown in its own garden plot (*gartine* means 'little field'), with organic eggs from its chickens. Along with break-fast dishes like scrambled eggs on sourdough with fresh herbs, it has sandwiches, salads and a sweet-and-savoury high tea of an afternoon. (gartine.nl)

De Laatste Kruimel

CAFE €

 15 MAP P46, C7

Opening to a tiny canal-side terrace and decorated with vintage finds from the Noordermarkt and wooden pallets upcycled as furniture, the 'Last Crumb' has glass display cases filled with pies, quiches, breads, cakes and scones. Grandmothers, children, couples on dates and just about everyone else crowds in for sweet treats and fantastic organic sandwiches. (delaatstekruimel.com)

Carstens Brasserie

DUTCH €€

 16 MAP P46, D2

The Netherlands' sea and meadows provide the produce used at this skylit restaurant, which champions local suppliers. À la carte and three- and four-course menus are super-seasonal, with meat, fish and vegetarian options (eg 'beet Wellington'). End with a plate of Dutch farmers' cheeses with nutbread. Even wines from abroad have Dutch links. (carstensbrasserie.nl)

Blue Amsterdam

CAFE €€

 17 MAP P46, B8

From this glass-walled cafe atop the Kalverpassage shopping centre, you'll have wraparound views over Amsterdam's historic centre. Its organic menu spans all-day breakfasts to sandwiches, burgers, soups and salads, as well as sweets such as brownies or custard tarts. Mimosas, Bloody Marys and sparkling wines are served as well as coffee and tea. (blue-amsterdam.nl)

Banketbakkerij Van der Linde

ICE CREAM €

 18 MAP P46, C4

A long line regularly snakes out the door of this narrow, generations-old shop where everyone is queuing for – wait for it – vanilla ice cream. That's the only flavour! But this vanilla is unlike any other: a soft, velvety sugar cloud almost like whipped cream in texture. Choose from cones, cups or ice-cream sandwiches. (020-624 8213)

Van Stapele Koekmakerij

BAKERY €

 19 MAP P46, A7

Van Stapele is a true specialist, baking just one thing and baking it well: Valrhona dark-chocolate

Van Wonderen Stroopwafels

FOKKE BAARSSEN/SHUTTERSTOCK ©

Chinatown

Amsterdam's small Chinatown centres on Zeedijk, the site of New Year celebrations (there's a lion dance on 2 January as well as Chinese New Year later in January or February). It's home to Europe's largest Chinese Imperial-style Buddhist temple, 2000-built **He Hua Temple** (Map p46, E4; ibps.nl), with its ornate 'mountain gate'.

There are Asian grocery stores and restaurants popular with locals including **Nam Kee** (Map p46, E4; namkee.nl), serving Cantonese classics, or **New King** (Map p46, E4; newking.nl), with dishes like salt-and-pepper prawns, Peking duck or numerous vegetarian choices.

cookies with a white-chocolate centre. The cookies are served warm and gooey straight from the oven, ensuring the teensy shop always smells heavenly. (vanstapele.com)

Van Wonderen Stroopwafels
BAKERY €

20 MAP P46, B8

Van Wonderen's scrumptious twists on classic Dutch *stroopwafels* (thin, waffles sandwiched with syrup) include *speculoos* (spiced biscuit), salted caramel, marshmallows, coconut or chocolate sprinkles. They're delectable when served warm to eat on the spot; you can also buy stacks of 10 *stroopwafels* wrapped in cellophane tied with ribbons, or beautifully stencilled tins that make great gifts. (vanwonderen stroopwafels.nl)

Drinking

Brouwerij De Prael
BREWERY

21 MAP P46, E3

Sample craft beers (Scotch ale, IPA, barley wine and many more varieties) from the socially minded De Prael brewery, known for employing people who have suffered mental illness. Its multilevel taproom has comfy couches and big wooden tables strewn about. There's often live music, comedy and quiz nights. (deprael.nl)

Café De Dokter
BROWN CAFE

22 MAP P46, B7

Candles flicker on the tables, old jazz records play in the background, and chandeliers and a birdcage hang from the ceiling at atmospheric De Dokter, which at 18 sq metres is allegedly Amsterdam's smallest pub. Whiskies and smoked beef sausage are specialities. A surgeon opened it in 1798, hence the name. The seventh generation of his family still runs it. (cafe-de-dokter.nl)

Cut Throat
BAR

23 MAP P46, D4

Beneath 1930s arched brick ceilings and chandeliers, Cut Throat cleverly combines a men's barbershop with a happening bar. The menu features Caribbean-inspired street food and tropical cocktails and popular bottomless brunches. Reservations for a trim or table are strongly recommended. (cutthroat barber.nl)

Hoppe BROWN CAFE

24 MAP P46, A8

An Amsterdam institution, Hoppe has been filling glasses since 1670. Barflies and raconteurs toss back brews amid the ancient wood panelling of the *bruin café* at No 18 and the more modern, early-20th-century pub at No 20. In all but the iciest weather, the energetic crowd spills out from the dark interior and onto the Spui. (cafehoppe.com)

In 't Aepjen BROWN CAFE

25 MAP P46, E3

Candles burn even during the day in this 15th-century building – one of two remaining wooden buildings in the city – which has been a tavern since 1519. In the 16th and 17th centuries it was an inn for sailors from the Far East, who often brought *aapjes* (monkeys) to trade for lodging. Vintage jazz on the stereo enhances the time-warp feel.

Tales & Spirits COCKTAIL BAR

26 MAP P46, B3

Chandeliers glitter beneath wooden beams at Tales & Spirits, which creates its own house infusions, syrups and vinegar-based shrubs. Cocktails such as Any Port in a Storm (Porter's gin, Sailor Jerry spiced rum, sorbet and jalapeño bitters) and the Van Gogh–inspired Drop of Art (with *oude jenever* and absinthe) are served in vintage and one-of-a-kind glasses. (talesand spirits.com)

't Mandje LGBTIQ+

27 MAP P46, F4

Amsterdam's oldest gay bar opened in 1927, then shut in 1982 when the Zeedijk grew too seedy.

Tasting Jenever

Jenever (ye-*nay*-ver; Dutch gin – also spelt *genever*) is made from juniper berries and is drunk chilled. It arrives in a tulip-shaped shot glass filled to the brim – tradition dictates that you bend over the bar, with your hands behind your back, and take a deep sip. Most people prefer smooth *jonge* (young) *jenever*; *oude* (old) *jenever* has a strong juniper flavour.

Centuries-old tasting houses where you can try *jenever* include **Wynand Fockink** (p43), **Proeflokaal de Ooievaar** (Map p46, E3; proe flokaaldeooievaar.nl) and **De Drie Fleschjes** (Map p46, B4; dedriefleschjes. nl). New-generation bar **Dutch Courage** (Map p46, E3; dutchcourage cocktails.com) celebrates *jenever* and old Dutch liqueurs.

But its trinket-covered interior was lovingly dusted every week until it reopened in 2008. Devoted bar-tenders can tell you about the bar's brassy lesbian founder Bet van Beeren. It's one of the most *gezellig* (cosy, convivial) places in the centre, gay or straight. (cafetmandje. amsterdam)

VOC Café
BROWN CAFE

28 MAP P46, F3

Inside the landmark 15th-century Schreierstoren, this atmospheric *café* (pub) has a historical interior with hefty timber beams and a canal-side terrace. *Jenevers*, liqueurs and local beers are served alongside classic bar snacks such as *bitterballen* (deep-fried meatballs) and huge, thin Dutch pancakes with sweet or savoury toppings. If you're arriving by boat you can dock at its pier. (schreierstoren.nl)

Bubbles & Wines
WINE BAR

29 MAP P46, C6

More than 55 wines are avail-able by the glass at this stylish wine and champagne bar, along with wine-tasting flights (three half-glasses grouped by grape, region or quality). All up there are over 700 varieties by the bottle plus some 400 champagnes, from both renowned and lesser-known champagne houses. Classy bar food includes caviar blinis, oysters, charcuterie and cheese platters. (bubblesandwines.com)

Entertainment

Bitterzoet
LIVE MUSIC

30 ⭐ MAP P46, C2

Always full, always changing, this venue with a capacity of just 350 people is one of the friendliest plac-es in town, with a diverse crowd. Music (sometimes live, sometimes courtesy of a DJ) can be funk, roots, drum 'n' bass, Latin, Afro-beat, old-school jazz or hip-hop groove. (bitterzoet.com)

Tobacco Theater
THEATRE

31 ⭐ MAP P46, C7

A 1900-built tobacco auction house now contains this architec-turally designed theatre, which stages dinner-and-cabaret shows in English and Dutch, and presents theatre productions and concerts. In addition to the 300-capacity theatre, it has an experimental art and concept room in the cellar, along with several lounge areas including a cocktail bar overlooking the stage, and an old bank vault. (tobaccotheater.nl)

De Brakke Grond
THEATRE

32 ⭐ MAP P46, C6

De Brakke Grond sponsors a fan-tastic array of music, experimental video, modern dance and exciting young theatre at its nifty perfor-mance hall in the Flemish Cultural Centre. Upcoming events are listed on its website. (brakkegrond.nl)

Shopping

X Bank
DESIGN

33 🔒 MAP P46, A5

More than just a concept store showcasing visionary haute couture and ready-to-wear fashion, furniture, art, gadgets and homewares by established and emerging Dutch designers, the 700-sq-metre X Bank also hosts exhibitions, workshops, launches and lectures. Interior displays change every month; check the website for upcoming events. (xbank.amsterdam)

Posthumus
STATIONERY

34 🔒 MAP P46, B6

Established in 1865, this wonderfully preserved shop with original timber cabinetry produces lacquer stamps for wax seals, brass branding stamps, shutter stamps for embossing and rubber hobby stamps in Dutch-themed designs such as gabled canal houses. Stamps can be made to order. It also has feathered, quill-like fountain pens and fine papers. (posthumuswinkel.nl)

Mark Raven Grafiek
GIFTS & SOUVENIRS

35 🔒 MAP P46, B4

Artist Mark Raven's distinctive vision of Amsterdam is available on posters, coasters, fridge magnets and well-cut T-shirts that make great souvenirs. Prices are impressively reasonable and there's often a sale rack out front. Climb the shop's spiral staircase to find a small gallery of large prints also on display. (markraven.nl)

Bonbon Boutique
JEWELLERY

36 🔒 MAP P46, B6

A white-on-white space is the backdrop for Amsterdam-designed jewellery crafted from gold, sterling silver, brass, precious stones and coloured crystal. All packaging is plastic-free. (bonbonboutique.nl)

By Popular Demand
GIFTS & SOUVENIRS

37 🔒 MAP P46, A5

Stop by this large, sunny shop for nifty gift-y wares. Cards, gadgets, lamps and other hip home decor stock the shelves. Many items are Amsterdam-inspired and make for easy-to-transport souvenirs – like

Posthumus

windmill or bicycle lapel pins, diaries, notebooks and Miffy tea towels plus rock'n'roll-inspired Delftware. (bpd.nu/nl)

Hempstory
CONCEPT STORE

38 🔒 MAP P46, D5

Everything at this light-filled contemporary boutique is made from industrial hemp: skincare ranges (including body washes such as hemp and ginseng), insect repellent, homewares (blankets, throws, cushions, botanical prints on hemp paper), men's and women's clothing (shirts, jackets, scarves, hats) and hemp-cord jewellery. Its tiny cafe serves (nonactive) hemp tea, hempseed cakes and hempseed smoothies. (hempstory.nl)

Condomerie het Gulden Vlies
ADULT

39 🔒 MAP P46, D4

In the heart of the Red Light District, this brightly lit store sells condoms in every imaginable size, colour, flavour and design (horned devils, Delftware tiles, tulips, Dutch orange...), along with various saucy gifts. Photos aren't allowed inside. (condomerie.com)

Magna Plaza
MALL

40 🔒 MAP P46, B4

This grand 19th-century landmark building, once the main post office, is now home to an upmarket shopping mall with boutiques stocking fashion, gifts and jewellery. (magnaplaza.nl)

Art & Book Markets

Save on gallery fees by buying direct from the artists at Amsterdam's Sunday art market, **Art Amsterdam Spui** (Map p46, B7; artamsterdam-spui.com). Some 60 artists set up on the square from March to December. Old tomes, maps and sheet music are the speciality at the daily (bar Sunday) **Oudemanhuispoort Book Market** (Map p46, D7) in an atmospheric covered alleyway.

De Bijenkorf
DEPARTMENT STORE

41 🔒 MAP P46, C5

Amsterdam's most fashionable department store has a grander exterior than interior, but it occupies the city's highest-profile location, facing the Royal Palace. Shoppers will enjoy the well-chosen clothing, cosmetics, accessories, toys, homewares and books. The snazzy cafe on the 5th floor has a terrace with steeple views. (debijenkorf.nl)

Rush Hour Records
MUSIC

42 🔒 MAP P46, B4

House and techno are the main genres on offer in this vast space, but funk, jazz, dubstep, electronica and disco fill the bins too. A favourite with DJs and multimedia artists, it's an excellent spot to find out what's going on in Amsterdam's dance-music scene. (rushhour.nl)

Walking Tour

Amsterdam's Beautiful Bridges

An incredible 1753 bridges cross Amsterdam's canals. This walk passes some of the city's most beautiful as they span the picturesque waterways. For more than four centuries the canals have performed the epic task of keeping Amsterdam above water, since they help drain the landscape. Today 100km of channels do their duty.

Getting There

Trams 4 & 14 stop nearby

This walk starts just north of Rembrandtplein and winds for 2.5km along and around the Amstel river, from which Amsterdam takes its name. Allow around two hours.

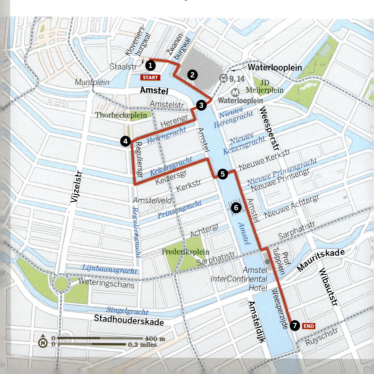

❶ Groenburgwal

Step out onto the white draw-bridge that crosses the **Groenburgwal** and look north. Many Amsterdammers swear this is the loveliest canal view of all – a pick backed by Impressionist Claude Monet, who painted it in 1874 as *The Zuiderkerk (South Church) Amsterdam: Looking up the Groenburgwal*.

❷ Stopera

Head to the **Stopera** building, Amsterdam's combination of city hall and **Nationale Opera & Ballet** (p159). Its terrace is a great place for watching the boats on the Amstel.

❸ Blauwbrug

Cross the river via the 1884 **Blauwbrug** (Blue Bridge). Inspired by Paris's Alexandre III bridge, it features tall, ornate street lamps topped by the imperial crown of Amsterdam, fish sculptures and foundations shaped like a medieval ship prow.

❹ Reguliersgracht

Walk along the Herengracht to **Reguliersgracht** (p89), the 'seven bridges' canal. Stand with your back to the Thorbeckeplein and the Herengracht directly in front of you and lean over the bridge to see seven humpbacked arches leading down the canal straight ahead.

❺ Magere Brug

Walk along the Keizersgracht and cross the wedding-photo-favourite (and star of films including the 1971 James Bond thriller *Diamonds Are Forever*), **Magere Brug** (Skinny Bridge). It has a hand-operated central section that can be raised to let boats through. The bridge is especially pretty at night, when it glows with 1200 tiny lights.

❻ Amstelsluizen

Continue south to the **Amstelsluizen**. These impressive locks, dating from 1674, allow the canals to be flushed with fresh water. The sluices on the city's west side are left open as the stagnant water is pumped out to sea.

❼ De Ysbreeker

Take Prof Tulpplein past the Inter-Continental Hotel to **De Ysbreeker** (deysbreeker.nl). Dating from 1702, it's named after a vessel that docked in front to break the ice on the river during the winter months (stained-glass windows illustrate the scene). Grab a seat on the enormous waterfront terrace to see what's gliding by these days.

Explore

Western Canal Ring & the Jordaan

Flowing west of the Medieval Centre, the glinting waterways of the Western Canal Ring are graced by grand old buildings and enticing speciality shops. Next door, the former workers' quarter of the Jordaan is one of Amsterdam's most intimate and engaging neighbourhoods, with candlelit bruin cafés (traditional Dutch pubs) and flower-box-adorned eateries spilling out onto its narrow streets.

The Short List

○ **Anne Frank Huis (p62)** *Contemplating the young diarist's brave life and tragic death where she and her family hid from the Nazis.*

○ **Negen Straatjes (p75)** *Browsing the speciality shops along these 'nine streets' criss-crossed by canals.*

○ **Westerkerk (p68)** *Catching an organ concert at this landmark church.*

○ **De Twee Zwaantjes (p73)** *Spending the evening in the Jordaan's cosy bruin cafés.*

Getting There & Around

🚶 This area's narrow streets and dense concentration of shops and restaurants make it ideal for exploring on foot.

🚊 Trams 13 and 17 run through the neighbourhood's centre; trams 3, 5, 7 and 19 skirt its western edge.

🚌 Buses 18, 21, 22 and 48 provide the quickest access from Centraal Station to the neighbourhood's north and west, and the Western Islands.

Neighbourhood Map on p66

View from Westerkerk (p68) HIGH FLIERS/SHUTTERSTOCK ©

Top Experience 📷

Glimpse the annexe behind the diary at Anne Frank Huis

It is one of the 20th century's most compelling stories: a young Jewish girl forced into hiding with her family and their friends to escape deportation by the Nazis. The building they used as a hideaway is one of Amsterdam's most important and profound sights.

🎯 MAP P66, D5

annefrank.org

The Residents

The Franks moved into the upper floors of the specially prepared rear of the building, along with another couple, the Van Pels (called the Van Daans in Anne's diary), and their son, Peter. Four months later, Fritz Pfeffer (called Mr Dussel in the diary) joined the household. Here they survived until they were betrayed to the Gestapo in August 1944.

Offices & Warehouse

The building originally held Otto Frank's pectin (a substance used in jam-making) business. On the lower floors you'll see the former offices of Victor Kugler, Otto's business partner, and the desks of Miep Gies, Bep Voskuijl and Jo Kleiman, all of whom worked in the office and provided food, clothing and other goods for the household. The museum shows multilingual news reels of WWII footage narrated using segments of Anne's diary.

Secret Annexe

The upper floors in the Achterhuis (rear house) contain the Secret Annexe, where the living quarters have been preserved in powerful austerity. As you enter Anne's small bedroom, you can still see the remnants of a young girl's dreams: the photos of Hollywood stars and postcards of the Dutch royal family she pasted on the wall.

The Diary

More haunting exhibits and videos await after you return to the front house – including Anne's red-plaid diary itself, sitting alone in its glass case. Watch the video of Anne's old schoolmate Hanneli Goslar, who describes encountering Anne at Bergen-Belsen. Read heartbreaking letters from Otto, the only Secret Annexe occupant to survive the concentration camps.

★ Top Tips

o All tickets must be pre-purchased online with set time slots, released every Tuesday for the following six weeks.

o Late opening hours mean you can have an early dinner at one of the many excellent nearby cafes, then spend the evening hours in Amsterdam's most moving sight – with fewer crowds and plenty of time to contemplate this remarkable young girl's life and legacy.

o Interior photography is not permitted.

o There are many stairs; only the modern museum is accessible for wheelchairs.

o The cafe and shop are only accessible to ticket holders.

✕ Take a Break

Overlooking the Prinsengracht, the **museum cafe** serves light lunches, snacks and drinks.

Nearby, **Bistro Amsterdam** (p72) is a charming spot for classic Dutch dishes.

Walking Tour 🚶

Shops of Western Canal Ring & the Jordaan

These are Amsterdam's prime neighbourhoods for offbeat shops selling items you'd find nowhere else. Velvet ribbons? Herb-spiced Gouda? Vintage jewellery? They're all here amid the Western Canal's quirky stores and the Jordaan's eclectic boutiques and markets. Everything is squashed into a grid of tiny lanes – a perfect place for a stroll.

Walk Facts

Start Antiekcentrum Amsterdam

End De Kat in de Wijngaert

Length 3.3km; two hours

❶ Antiqueing at Antiekcentrum

Anyone who likes peculiar old stuff might enter **Antiekcentrum Amsterdam** (Amsterdam Antique Centre; antiekcentrumamsterdam.nl), a knick-knack mini-mall, and never come out.

❷ Crate Digging for Vinyl

Sift through stacks of vintage vinyl, CDs, posters, magazines and merchandise at **Second Life Music** (secondlifemusic.nl). Genres span blues, funk, house, metal and classical from all corners of the globe.

❸ Tunes at Johnny Jordaanplein

The small square **Johnny Jordaanplein** is dedicated to the local hero and musician who sang the romantic music known as *levenslied* (tears-in-your-beer-style ballads).

❹ Retro Threads

On Huidenstraat, in the shop-filled **Negen Straatjes** (p75), **Zipper** (zippervintageclothing.com) sells vintage clothing, footwear and accessories from the 1950s to the 1980s. Browse for trench coats, fleece-lined suede jackets, patterned shirts, sunglasses, shoes, hats and a rotating array of other treasures.

❺ Wearable Art

One-of-a-kind designs are printed on organic cotton T-shirts, hoodies and bandanas and sold at **Collect the Label** (collectthelabel.com), a gallery-style white-walled space that's a curated collective of local artists.

❻ Historic Workwear

A vestige of the Jordaan's workers-quarter roots, **De Mof** (demof kleding.nl) has been selling durable work- and casualwear here since 1885 (look for the Royal Warrant plaque out front). Historical collections provide inspiration for its Waddenzee fisher's jumpers, coal workers' black jackets, and overalls with embroidered patches.

❼ Relax at De Kat in de Wijngaert

With gorgeous stained glass, cosy **De Kat in de Wijngaert** (dekatin dewijngaert.nl) is the kind of *bruin café* where you can easily find yourself settling in for a while.

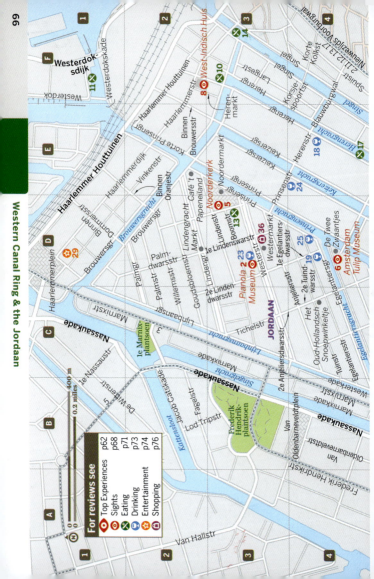

Western Canal Ring & the Jordaan

F Westerdoksdijk

Westerdok

11

Haarlemmer Houttuinen

Haarlemmerdijk

Haarlemmer Houttuinen

Binnen Dommerstr

Binnen Prinsenstr

Vinkenstr

Binnen Oranjestr

Brouwersgr

Brouwersgr

Palm-dwarsstr

Palmgr

Palmstr

Willemsstr

Goudsbloemstr

Lindengracht

't Markt

Café 't Papeneiland

Noorderkerk

Prinsengr

Keizersgr

Herenstr

Herenstr

Herenmarkt

Langestr

Korte Langestr

Singel

Spuistr

Korte Kolkst

Nieuwezijds Voorburgwal

Haarlemmerstr

Haarlemmerstr

Binnen Brouwersstr

Korte Prinsengr

Noordermarkt

Keizersgr

8 West-Indisch Huis

14

10

5

13

1e Lindenstr

1e Lindendwarsstr

1e Lindenstr

Boomstr

2e Linden-dwarsstr

Pianola Museum

23

2

Westerstr

Westermarkt

1e Egelantiers-dwarsstr

1e Tuin-dwarsstr

36

24

25

19

6

De Twee Zwaantjes

Amsterdam Tulip Museum

Herengracht

17

18

Keizersgr

Prinsengr

Prinsengr

Egelantiersgr

Anjeliersstr

2e Anjeliersdwarsstr

JORDAAN

Het Oud-Hollandsch Snoepwinkeltje

Anjeliersstr

2e Tuindwarsstr

Tichelstr

Lijnbaansgr

Lijnbaansgr

Marnixstr

Egelantiersstr

Tuinstr

Egelantiersgr

Nassaukade

Nassaukade

29

Haarlemmerplein

Binnen Dommerstr

Brouwersgr

1e Marnixplantsoen

1e Nassaustr

De Wittenstr

Marnixstr

Marnixkade

Marnixkade

Frederik Hendrikplantsoen

Van Oldenbarneveldstr

Nassaukade

Nassaukade

3e Marnixstr

Kattensloot

Jacob Catskade

Fagelstr

Lod Tripstr

Van Hallstr

Frederik Hendrikstr

Van Oldenbarneveldstr

Westerdok

400 m

0.2 miles

For reviews see

Top Experiences	p62
Sights	p68
Eating	p71
Drinking	p73
Entertainment	p74
Shopping	p76

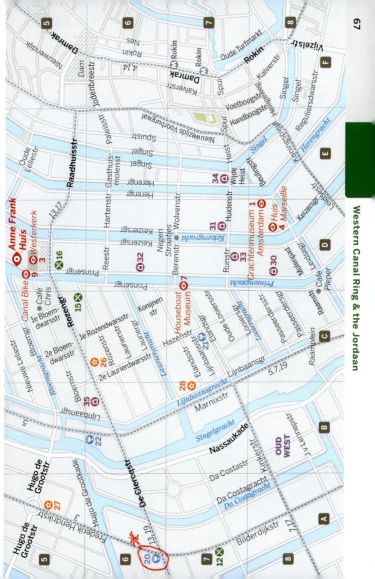

Sights

Grachtenmuseum Amsterdam

MUSEUM

1 ⊙ MAP P66, D8

Learn about the remarkable feats of engineering behind the Canal Ring through this museum's holograms, videos, models, cartoons, scale model of Amsterdam and other innovative exhibits, which explain how the canals and the houses that line them were built. Unlike at most Amsterdam museums, you can't simply wander through: small groups go in together to experience the multimedia exhibits. It takes about 45 minutes, and you'll come out knowing why Amsterdam's houses tilt. Admission includes an audioguide. (Museum of the Canals; grachten.museum)

Pianola Museum

MUSEUM

2 ⊙ MAP P66, D3

This is a very special place, crammed with pianolas from the early 1900s. The museum has around 50, although only a dozen are on display at any given time, as well as some 40,000 music rolls and a player pipe organ. It's open Friday, Saturday and Sunday afternoons for continuous tours, or by appointment. Regular concerts are held on the player pianos, featuring anything from Mozart to Fats Waller and rare classical or jazz tunes composed specially for the instrument. (pianolamuseum.online)

Westerkerk

CHURCH

3 ⊙ MAP P66, D5

The main gathering place for Amsterdam's Dutch Reformed community, this church was built for rich Protestants to a 1621 design by Hendrick de Keyser. Rembrandt (1606–69), who died bankrupt at nearby Rozengracht, was buried in a pauper's grave somewhere in the church. Lunchtime organ concerts lasting around 30 minutes take place at 1pm most Wednesdays. Its bell tower, the **Westertoren**, will resume carillon recitals and tower climbs with panoramic views following renovations expected to be completed in 2024. (Western Church; westerkerk.nl)

Huis Marseille

MUSEUM

4 ⊙ MAP P66, D8

This photography museum stages large-scale temporary exhibitions from its own collection as well as travelling shows. Themes might include portraiture, nature or regional photography. Its gallery spaces spread over two 17th-century canal houses, including Huis Marseille, built around 1665 by French merchant Isaac Focquier, who installed a map of the French port Marseille on the facade. Stucco-work and Jacob de Wit's ceiling painting were added the following century; the 18th-century garden house was reconstructed in 2003. (huismarseille.nl)

Noorderkerk

CHURCH

5 MAP P66, D3

Near the Prinsengracht's northern end, this imposing Calvinist church was completed in 1623 for the 'common' people in the Jordaan. (The upper classes attended the Westerkerk further south.) It was built in the shape of a broad Greek cross (four arms of equal length) around a central pulpit, giving the entire congregation unimpeded access. Hendrick de Keyser's design, unusual at the time, would become common for Protestant churches throughout the country. It hosts the well-regarded Saturday-afternoon Noorderkerkconcerten concert series. (Northern Church; noorderkerk.org)

Amsterdam Tulip Museum

MUSEUM

6 MAP P66, D4

Allow around half an hour at this diminutive museum, which offers an overview of the history of the country's favourite bloom. Through exhibits, timelines and two short films (in English), you'll learn how Ottoman merchants encountered the flowers in the Himalayan steppes and began commercial production in Turkey, how fortunes were made and lost during Dutch 'Tulipmania' in the 17th century, and how bulbs were used as food during WWII. You'll also discover present-day growing and harvesting techniques. (amsterdamtulipmuseum.com)

Amsterdam Tulip Museum

EQROY/SHUTTERSTOCK ©

Amsterdam's Engineering Marvels

Far from being simply decorative, or even waterways for transport, the city's ingeniously conceived canals were crucial to drain and reclaim the waterlogged land. They solved Amsterdam's essential problem: keeping the land and sea separate.

Core Canals

Amsterdam's core canals include the singular **Singel**, originally a moat that defended Amsterdam's outer limits. Beyond it is the **Herengracht** (Gentlemen's Canal), where Amsterdam's wealthiest residents built their mansions, particularly around the Golden Bend. Almost as swanky was the **Keizersgracht** (Emperor's Canal), a nod to Holy Roman Emperor Maximilian I.

The **Prinsengracht** – named after William the Silent, Prince of Orange and the first Dutch royal – had smaller residences and warehouses. It acted as a barrier against the working-class Jordaan beyond.

Radial Canals

Cutting across the core canals like spokes on a bicycle wheel are the radial canals. The **Brouwersgracht** (Brewers Canal) is one of Amsterdam's most beautiful waterways. It takes its name from the many breweries that lined the banks in the 16th and 17th centuries.

The **Leidsegracht** is named after the city of Leiden, to which it was the main water route, while peaceful **Reguliersgracht** was named after an order of monks whose monastery was located nearby.

Houseboat Museum MUSEUM

 MAP P66, D7

The 23m-long *Hendrika Maria*, a former cargo ship from 1914, offers a good sense of how *gezellig* (cosy, convivial) life can be on the water. A map lets you navigate its interior; the actual displays are minimal, but you can watch a presentation on houseboats (some pretty and some ghastly) and inspect the sleeping, living, cooking and dining quarters with all the mod cons. It's closed Mondays year-round and Tuesdays and Wednesdays November to February. (houseboatmuseum.nl)

West-Indisch Huis HISTORIC BUILDING

 MAP P66, F2

Built in 1617 as a meat market and militia barracks, this historical building was rented by the Dutch West India Company (Geoctroyeerde West-Indische Compagnie; GWC) as its headquarters in 1623.

It was here that the GWC's governors signed off on the construction of a fort on the island of Manhattan in 1625, establishing New Amsterdam (now New York City).

Canal Bike BOATING

 9 MAP P66, D5

These 'canal bike' pedal boats, seating up to four people, allow you to splash around the canals at your own speed. In addition to this location adjacent to the Anne Frank Huis, it has three other departure points (by the Rijksmuseum, Leidseplein and Keizersgracht). The operator, Stromma, can also arrange electric-boat rental and runs various canal cruises around Amsterdam. (stromma.com)

Eating

De Belhamel EUROPEAN €€

 10 MAP P66, F3

In warm weather, the canal-side tables here at the head of the Herengracht are enchanting, and the richly wallpapered split-level Art Nouveau interior provides a romantic backdrop for French-influenced dishes such as tenderloin steak tartare with black truffles or halibut with roast Jerusalem artichoke and Dutch mussels. (belhamel.nl)

Wolf Atelier GASTRONOMY €€€

11 MAP P66, F1

Atop a 1920 railway swing bridge, a glass box with pivoting windows is the showcase for experimental chef Michael Wolf's four, five and 15-course tasting menus featuring unexpected Asian and European flavour combinations such as, mango and radish or Lapsang Souchong–tea-smoked sea bass. The 360-degree views are magical at night. (wolfatelier.nl)

nNea PIZZA €€

12 MAP P66, A7

Ranked in the 50 Top Pizza World list (and in Europe's top 10), nNea's bright-yellow woodfire oven takes pride of place, cooking high-crusted Neapolitan pizzas with both traditional and contemporary toppings such as yellow-plum-tomato sauce, Padrón peppers, smoked mozzarella and homemade nduja salami. Wine pairings are available; you can also order pizzas to take away. (nneapizza.com)

Winkel 43 CAFE €

13 MAP P66, D3

This sprawling, indoor-outdoor space is great for people-watching. It's popular at all hours, from breakfast through to evening drinks, but the real reason everyone's here is its tall, cakey *appeltaart* (apple pie), with clouds of whipped cream. On market days (Monday and Saturday), there's almost always a queue out the door. (winkel43.nl)

Stubbe's Haring SEAFOOD €

14 MAP P66, F3

Overlooking the Singel, footsteps from Centraal Station, Stubbe's open-air fish stall has been a major source of pickled herring for Amsterdammers for more than a century. You can eat it straight up or on a bread roll; just be sure to sprinkle it with diced onion first.

Bonboon

VEGAN €€

15 MAP P66, C5

In bright Rozenstraat premises with herringbone timber floors, beautiful tiles, big picture windows and striking lighting, Bonboon crafts artful vegan cuisine in its open kitchen. Four- and five-course menus might feature smoked cauliflower with rosewater harissa, lacquered aubergine with mint and curry leaf, or fermented radicchio with candied walnut and tahini dressing. Finish with hazelnut frangipane cake with apple-miso caramel. (bonboon.nl)

Bistro Amsterdam

DUTCH €€

16 MAP P66, D5

If you're not in town visiting your Dutch *oma* (grandma), try the honest-to-goodness cooking at this charming retro bistro instead. Classics include *stamppot* (potatoes mashed with vegetables) with sausage, *raasdonders* (split peas with bacon, onion and pickles) and *poffertjes* (small pancakes with butter and powdered sugar). Warm sandwiches are available at lunch. House-made liqueurs include plum and *drop* (liquorice) varieties. (bistroamsterdam.nl)

Miss G's Brunch Boat

BRUNCH €€

17 MAP P66, E4

A winning combination, Miss G's Brunch Boat takes a two-hour cruise through Amsterdam's canals while serving weekend brunch (freshly shucked oysters, loaded waffles, burritos, eggs Benedict), with bottomless options – drinks include five types of Bloody Marys. (missgs.nl)

All Sorts of Liquorice

The Dutch love their sweets, the most famous of which is *drop,* the word for all varieties of liquorice. It may be gummy-soft or tough as leather and shaped like coins or miniature cars, but the most important distinction is between *zoete* (sweet) and *zoute* (salty). The latter is often an alarming surprise, even for avowed fans of the black stuff. But with such a range of textures and additional flavours – mint, honey, laurel – even liquorice sceptics might be converted.

Charming **Het Oud-Hollandsch Snoepwinkeltje** (Map p66, C4; snoepwinkeltje.com), with apothecary jars filled with flavours ranging from chocolate to coffee, cardamom and honey, and all manner of fruit, is a good place to do a taste test.

Drinking Bastions of Jordaan

A certain hard-drinking, hard-living spirit persists from the days when the Jordaan burst with 80,000 residents (compared with today's 20,000) and *bruin cafés* functioned as a refuge from the slings and arrows of workaday life.

Establishments still going strong include **De Twee Zwaantjes** (Map p66, D4; cafedetweezwaantjes.nl) (which is at its hilarious best on Wednesday nights when patrons and staff belt out classic Dutch tunes) and the Jordaan's oldest *bruin café*, **Café Chris** (Map p66, C5), opened in 1624 (workers building the Westertoren collected their pay here). The name of 1642 gem **Café 't Papeneiland** (Map p66, E2; papeneiland.nl) goes back to the Reformation, when it was reached via a secret tunnel to a clandestine Catholic church. Low-ceilinged **Café Pieper** (Map p66, C8) hails from 1665.

Drinking

't Arendsnest BROWN CAFE

18 MAP P66, E4

With glowing copper *jenever* (Dutch gin) boilers behind the bar, this gorgeous *bruin café* only serves Dutch beer: 50 rotate on tap, with over 100 by the bottle, sourced from 400 Dutch breweries. It also has more than 40 *jenevers*, ciders, whiskies and liqueurs, all of which are Dutch too. (arendsnest.nl)

't Smalle BROWN CAFE

19 MAP P66, D4

Dating back to 1786 as a *jenever* distillery and tasting house, and restored during the 1970s with antique porcelain beer pumps and lead-framed windows, this locals' favourite is one of Amsterdam's most charming *bruin cafés*. Dock your boat right by the pretty stone terrace, which is wonderfully convivial by day and impossibly romantic at night. (t-smalle.nl)

Monks Coffee Roasters COFFEE

20 MAP P66, A6

Monks sources and roasts outstanding coffee; its house blend, prepared with a variety of brewing methods, is phenomenal. The bare-boards space is brilliant for brunch (try the avocado toast or banana bread). (monkscoffee.nl)

Bar Oldenhof COCKTAIL BAR

21 MAP P66, C7

Ring the doorbell to enter this fabulously atmospheric speakeasy. Set over three levels, it evokes the roaring 1920s with dimly lit dark-wood panelling, velvet armchairs and a monthly changing cocktail menu and jazz soundtrack. (bar-oldenhof.nl)

Cafe Soundgarden · BAR

22 · MAP P66, B6

In this grungy all-ages dive bar, the 'Old Masters' are the Ramones and Black Sabbath. Somehow a handful of pool tables, 1980s and '90s pinball machines, unkempt DJs and lovably surly bartenders add up to ineffable magic. Bands occasionally make an appearance, and the waterfront terrace scene is more like an impromptu party in someone's backyard. (cafesoundgarden.nl)

Sins of Sal · COCKTAIL BAR

23 · MAP P66, D3

Inspired by the cult Quentin Tarantino film *From Dusk Till Dawn*, this dark, vampire-themed Latin cocktail den creates concoctions from spirits such as mezcal and tequila with ingredients including cactus leaf, smoked chillies and purple corn, accompanied by spicy dishes like roasted bone-marrow nachos, oysters with fermented hot sauce or soft-shell-crab tacos. (sinsofsal.nl)

JD William's Whisky Bar · BAR

24 · MAP P66, E4

Over 250 whiskies from as far afield as Japan, New Zealand and South America are served on the rocks (with JD-motif ice cubes), neat or in seasonal cocktails at this whisky specialist. There are also craft beers and wines, as well as Asian sharing plates (pork ribs, kimchi croquettes or tempeh spring rolls). (jdwilliamswhiskybar.com)

Café P 96 · BROWN CAFE

25 · MAP P66, D4

If you don't want the night to end, P 96 is an amiable hangout. When most other *cafés* (pubs) in the Jordaan shut down for the night, this is where everyone ends up, rehashing their evening and striking up conversations with strangers. In summertime, head to the terrace across the street aboard a houseboat. (p96.nl)

Entertainment

Boom Chicago · COMEDY

26 · MAP P66, C6

Boom Chicago stages seriously funny improv-style comedy shows in English that make fun of Dutch

Performers at Boom Chicago

Shopping Streets

The **Negen Straatjes** (Nine Streets; Map p66, D7; de9straatjes.nl) represent a delightfully dense concentration of consumer pleasures. These 'nine little streets' are indeed small, each just a block long. The shops are tiny too, with numerous new and vintage fashion boutiques as well as highly specialised stores. The streets – from west to east, and north to south: Reestraat, Hartenstraat, Gasthuismolensteeg, Berenstraat, Wolvenstraat, Oude Spiegelstraat, Runstraat, Huidenstraat, Wijde Heisteeg – form a grid bounded by Prinsengracht to the west and Singel to the east.

To the north, the Haarlemmerbuurt is a legacy of the Brouwersgracht's former shipyards, breweries and warehouses. Its spine stretches along **Haarlemmerstraat**; across the Prinsengracht, its western extension, the **Haarlemmerdijk** continues to the Haarlemmerplein. Today, the long thoroughfare is lined with independent food and fashion boutiques, with an increasingly sustainable focus.

culture, American culture and everything that gets in the crosshairs. Edgier shows happen in the smaller upstairs theatre. The on-site bar helps fuel the festivities with buckets of ice and beer. You can also book in for two-hour comedy classes (also in English). (boom chicago.nl)

De Nieuwe Anita   ARTS CENTRE

27 ⭐ MAP P66, A5

This living-room venue, in a former school building and squat, is now a great *café* (pub) for the wild rock 'n' roller at heart. In the back, behind the bookcase-concealed door, the main room has a stage and screens cult movies (in English). DJs, comedy shows, quiz nights and vegetarian dinner parties are also on the eclectic agenda. (denieuweanita.nl)

Maloe Melo   BLUES

28 ⭐ MAP P66, B7

This is the freewheeling, fun-loving altar of Amsterdam's tiny blues scene. Music ranges from funk and soul to Texas blues and rockabilly. The cover charge is usually around €7.50; some performances are free. (maloemelo.com)

Movies   CINEMA

29 ⭐ MAP P66, D1

Amsterdam's oldest cinema dates to 1912. It is a *gezellig* gem, screening indie films alongside mainstream flicks in gorgeous art-deco surrounds. Go early for a pre-film tipple at the inviting *café*. (themovies.nl)

Shopping

Frozen Fountain
HOMEWARES

30 🔒 MAP P66, D8

Frozen Fountain is Amsterdam's best-known showcase of furniture and interior design. Prices are not cheap, but the daring designs are offbeat and very memorable (find a birthday gift for the impossible-to-wow friend). Best of all, it's an unpretentious place where you can browse at length without feeling uncomfortable. (frozenfountain.com)

Marie-Stella-Maris
COSMETICS

31 🔒 MAP P66, D7

Marie-Stella-Maris donates a percentage from every purchase of its plant-based skincare products and home fragrances to support sustainable water initiatives in 14 different countries. You might recognise its signature scent, Objets d'Amsterdam (made of green tea, bergamot and citrus), from one of many local hotels and restaurants, and it also makes a great gift. (marie-stella-maris.com)

360 Volt
HOMEWARES

32 🔒 MAP P66, D6

360 Volt sells industrial lighting – restored to create a quintessentially *gezellig* ambience while meeting energy-efficient international standards. Its lights grace some of the world's hottest restaurants, hotels and film sets. Here, in the showroom, you can check out displays for online ordering. Changing collections include scissor lights, tripods, suspended floor pendants,

Stamps, Noordermarkt

Neighbourhood Markets

Saturday's **Lindengracht Markt** (Map p66, D2; jordaanmarkten.nl) is a wonderfully authentic local affair, with bountiful fresh produce and delicacies including cheese, as well as clothing and homewares. Arrive as early as possible for the best pickings and fewest crowds.

Another good market for treasure hunters is Monday morning's **Westermarkt** (Map p66, D3; jordaanmarkten.nl), where bargain-priced clothing and fabrics are sold at 150 stalls; note it isn't in fact on Westermarkt but on Westerstraat, just near the **Noordermarkt** (Map p66, E3; jordaanmarkten.nl), which hosts a Monday-morning flea market and Saturday-morning *boerenmarkt* (farmers market).

work lights, wall lights, desk lamps and speciality bulbs. (360volt.com)

De Kaaskamer FOOD

33 MAP P66, D7

The name means 'the cheese room' and De Kaaskamer is indeed stacked to the rafters with over 400 different Dutch and organic varieties, as well as olives, tapenades, salads and other picnic ingredients. You can try before you buy or pick up a cheese-filled baguette to go. Vacuum-packing is available to take cheeses home. (kaaskamer.nl)

Anna + Nina JEWELLERY

34 🔒 MAP P66, E7

This atelier from local jewellery designer Anna + Nina sells dainty and minimalistic pieces. Book an appointment online with the in-house goldsmith to design your own ornament or invest in a 'never-ending bracelet' fused together with a special machine so it never comes off. (anna-nina.nl)

Urban Cacao CHOCOLATE

35 🔒 MAP P66, B6

Chocolatier, patissier and glacier Hans Mekking is the mastermind behind Urban Cacao. Filled with his chocolate bars, truffles and pralines using fair-trade beans (with sugar-free varieties), the stylish space also has colourful macarons (such as passion fruit and chocolate, mandarin and basil, and orange and gold dust for King's Day), plus ice cream in summer and hot chocolate in winter. (urban cacao.com)

Mechanisch Speelgoed TOYS

36 🔒 MAP P66, D3

This adorable shop is crammed full of nostalgic toys, including snow domes, glow lamps, masks, finger puppets and wind-up toys. And who doesn't need a good rubber chicken every once in a while? (mechanisch-speelgoed.nl)

Walking Tour

Wander Westerpark & Western Islands

A reedy wilderness, a post-industrial culture complex and a drawbridge-filled adventure await those who make the trip here. Architectural and creative hot spots add to the hip, eco-urban mash-up. The area's rags-to-riches story is prototypical Amsterdam: abandoned factory-land hits the skids, squatters salvage it, and it rises again in style.

Getting There

Tram 3 passes the area

Bus 22 goes to Het Schip

This area borders the Jordaan to the northwest; it's a 4km walk in all. Allow around three hours (you can also cycle the route).

❶ Architecture

Remarkable housing project **Het Schip** (hetschip.nl) is the pinnacle of Amsterdam School architecture. Michel de Klerk designed the triangular block, loosely resembling a ship, for railway employees. There is a small museum.

❷ Patch of Green

The pond-dappled green space **Westerpark** is a cool-cat hangout that blends into **Westergas** (westergas.nl), a former gasworks transformed into a cultural park, with *cafés* (pubs), theatres, breweries and other creative spaces.

❸ Terrace Drinks

On sunny afternoons, young professionals flock to the massive outdoor terrace at **Westergasterras** (westergasterras.nl), overlooking reed-filled ponds and a weir. A toasty fireplace also makes the indoors inviting.

❹ Digital Art

Wander over to the digital art centre **Fabrique des Lumières** (fabrique-lumieres.com). Here, classical and modern art come to life with projections blasted across the industrial walls with immersive musical soundtracks.

❺ City Gate

Once a defensive gateway to the city, the **Haarlemmerpoort** marked the start of the journey to Haarlem. The neoclassical structure, with Roman-temple-styled Corinthian pillars, was finished just in time for King William II's staged entry for his 1840 investiture.

❻ Western Islands

Cross the narrow drawbridge **Drieharingenbrug** (Three Herrings Bridge) to the **Western Islands**. Originally home to shipworks and the Dutch West India Company's warehouses in the early 1600s, the district is a world unto itself, cut through with canals.

❼ Scenic Zandhoek

Visit photogenic **Zandhoek**, a stretch of waterfront on the eastern shore. Now a yacht harbour, back in the 17th century it was a 'sand market' where ships would purchase bags of the stuff for ballast.

❽ Waterfront Chilling

End your walk dockside looking over the Western Islands' waterways from the sunny, south-facing terrace of **Hoogendam** (hoogendam.nl), a great place for a beer or homemade grapefruit lemonade with street-food snacks.

Explore ✦
Southern Canal Ring

A horseshoe-shaped loop of parallel canals, the Southern Canal Ring is home to the nightlife hubs of Leidseplein and Rembrandtplein. Between the two squares, the waterways are lined by some of the city's most elegant canal houses, some fine museums, a flower market and waterside restaurants and bars.

The Short List

○ **H'ART (p86)** *Catching blockbuster exhibitions in collaboration with world-famous art institutions.*

○ **Golden Bend (p83)** *Ambling alongside Golden Age canal-side properties.*

○ **Reguliersgracht (p89)** *Enjoying romantic views on the 'canal of seven bridges'.*

○ **Museum Van Loon (p87)** *Appreciating the lavish lifestyle of Amsterdam's top rung at this grand canal house.*

○ **Museum Willet-Holthuysen (p86)** *Exploring patrician waterside life in this historic home.*

Getting There & Around

🚋 This area is well served by trams. For the Leidseplein area, take tram 1, 2, 5, 7, 11, 12 or 19. To reach Rembrandtplein, take tram 4, which travels down Utrechtsestraat, or tram 14. Tram 24 cuts through the centre of the neighbourhood down busy Vijzelstraat.

Ⓜ Line 52 between Amsterdam Noord and Station Zuid stops at Vijzelgracht.

Neighbourhood Map on p84

Leidseplein (p87)

Walking Tour 🥾

Southern Canal Ring Stroll

Puttin' on the Ritz is nothing new to the Southern Canal Ring. Most of the area was built at the end of the 17th century when Amsterdam was wallowing in Golden Age cash. A wander through reveals grand mansions, swanky antique shops, an indulgent patisserie and a one-of-a-kind kitty museum. And while it's all stately, it's certainly not snobby.

Walk Facts

Start Flower Market
End Café Americain
Length 2km; 1½ hours

❶ Flower Market

The canal-side **Bloemenmarkt** (Flower Market) has been here since 1860. Exotic bulbs are the main stock, though cut flowers brighten the stalls, too.

❷ Golden Bend Riches

During the Golden Age, the Herengracht's **Golden Bend** was where the wealthiest Amsterdammers lived. Many mansions here date from the 1660s; the gables were allowed to be twice as wide as the standard Amsterdam model.

❸ Feline Art at the Kattenkabinet

The only Golden Bend abode that's open to the public is the **Kattenkabinet** (Cat Cabinet; kattenkabinet.nl), an offbeat museum devoted to cat-related art. A Picasso drawing, kitschy kitty lithographs and odd pieces of ephemera cram the creaky old house. Happy live kitties lounge on the window seats.

❹ City History at Amsterdam's Archives

Fascinating archive gems, such as a letter from Charles Darwin to Artis Royal Zoo in 1868, can be viewed in the tiled basement vault of the **Stadsarchief** (Municipal Archives; amsterdam.nl/stadsarchief), in a 1923 striped former bank.

❺ Treats at Patisserie Holtkamp

At **Patisserie Holtkamp** (patisserieholtkamp.nl), look up to spot the gilded royal coat of arms. This posh bakery supplies the Dutch royals with delicacies including *kroketten* (croquettes) with fillings of prawns, lobster and veal.

❻ Spiegel Quarter Antiques

The perfect Delft vase or 16th-century wall map will most assuredly be hiding among the antique stores, bric-a-brac shops and commercial art galleries in the Spiegel Quarter. **Hoogkamp Antiquariaat** (Prints & Maps Hoogkamp; fineartprints.nl) has wonderful prints of Amsterdam.

❼ Theatre Time

The neo-Renaissance **Internationaal Theater Amsterdam** (ita.nl), built in 1894, is used for large-scale plays, operettas and more.

❽ Drinks at Café Americain

Opened in 1902, Art Nouveau **Café Americain** (cafeamericain.nl) has huge stained-glass windows overlooking Leidseplein, a lovely, library-like reading table and a great terrace.

A B C D

Rokin

1 Oude Looiersstr
Huidenstr
Spui Spui
Looiersgr
Rokin 4, 14
Passeerdersstr
Prinsengr
Keizersgr
Herengr
Singel
Singel
Muntplein
Passeerdersgr
Molenpad
Leidsegr
Leidsestr
Singel
Taboo Bar

2 Raamstr
Leidsegracht
Keizersgracht
2, 11, 12
Singel
Herengr
Reguliersdwarsstr
Herengr
Club NYX
Blend XL
B'Femme
18
26
Prinsengracht
Kerkstr
Keizersgr
Nieuwe Spiegelstr
Vijzelstr
Korte Leidsedwarsstr
Leidsegr
Prinsengr
Church
Amsterdam Pipe Museum
42
40

3 Marnixstr
5, 7, 19
Leidseplein
30
6
35
9
32
33
25
44
Lijnbaansgr
Leidsekade
Leidsebosje
16
Lange Leidsedwarsstr
Prinsengr
Kerkstr
38
17

Hirschpassage
Max Euweplein
Leidsekruisstr
23
Spiegelgr
11
1e Weteringdwarsstr
19
31
Ziseniskade
Lijnbaansgr
Lijnbaansgracht
21
2e Weteringdwarsstr
Weteringlaan
Vijzelgr

4 Zandpad
Vondelpark
Vossiusstr
Singelgracht
Stadhouderskade
Weteringschans 1, 7, 19
Nieuwe Weteringstr
27

PC Hooftstr
Rijksmuseum
Boerenwetering
Weteringcircuit
14

5 Jan Luijkenstr
Paulus Potterstr
OUD ZUID

6 Honthorststr
Museumplein
Van Baerlestr
Johannes Vermeerstr
Museumpl
Hobbemakade
Ruysdaelkade
Frans Halsstr
Quellijnstr
1, 7, 19
1e Van der Helststr

A B C D

Southern Canal Ring

Map labels:

E F G H

Nieuwe Doelenstr
Kloveniersburgwal
Kloveniersburgwal
Groenburgwal
Zwanenburgwal
Zwanenburgwal
Zwanenburgwal
Waterlooplein
Jodenbreestr
Valkenburgerstr
Rapenburgerstr

1

Stopera
Muiderstr

Binnen Amstel
Halvemaansteeg
39
Amstel
Waterlooplein
14
Weesperstr

Reguliersbreestr
Bakkerstr
Montmartre
Amstelstr
Museum of the Mind /
Outsider Art
2

29
10
7
Rembrandtplein
8 Our House
5

24
Reguliersdwarsstr
2
Museum Willet-
Holthuysen
1 H'ART

22
15
43
Herengr
Herengr

Thorbeckeplein
Reguliersgracht
Utrechtsestr
Keizersgr
Keizersgr
Nieuwe Keizersgr
Nieuwe Keizersgr
Nieuwe Kerkstr

4 Foam
Keizersgr
Keizersgracht
Amstel
Magere
Brug
3

3
Museum
Van Loon
Keizersgr
37
Kerkstr
Nieuwe
Prinsengracht

Reguliersgr
Prinsengr
41
Prinsengr
Lepelstr

Prinsengr
Prinsengr
Prinsengracht
34
Nieuwe Achtergr

Amstelveld
Utrechtsestr
4

Noorderstr
Utrechtsedwarsstr
12
28
36
Achtergr
Amstel
13

Nieuwe Looiersstr
Fokke Simonszstr
Falckstr
Sarphatistr

Weteringschans
Frederiksplein
Sarphatistr
Oostende
Sarphatistr
5

1,7,19
Westeinde

Den Texstr
Sarphatikade
Singelgracht

Nicolaas Witsenkade
N 0 / 0
200 m
0.1 miles

Stadhouderskade
Hemonylaan
Van Woustr

For reviews see

	Sights	p86
	Eating	p88
	Drinking	p91
	Entertainment	p93
	Shopping	p94

Quellijnstr
Gerard Doustr
Albert Cuypstr
Govert Flinckstr
2e Jan Steenstr

6

E F G H

Sights

H'ART
MUSEUM

1 ◎ MAP P84, G2

Following the Russian invasion of Ukraine, Amsterdam's branch of St Petersburg's State Hermitage Museum severed ties, instead forming new partnerships with France's Centre Pompidou, the British Museum and Smithsonian American Art Museum. Now known as H'ART, its changing exhibitions span historic bibliographies to single important topics (such as the context of slavery) along with blockbusters like 2025's Leiden Collection collaboration to celebrate Amsterdam's 750th birthday. Its inner courtyard hosts Saturday produce markets and an open-air summer cinema. (hartmuseum.nl)

Museum Willet-Holthuysen
MUSEUM

2 ◎ MAP P84, F2

This exquisite canal house was built in 1687 for Amsterdam mayor Jacob Hop, then remodelled in 1739. It's named after Louisa Willet-Holthuysen, who inherited it from her coal-and-glass-merchant father and lived a lavish, bohemian life here with her husband Abraham. She bequeathed it to the city in 1895. Now run by the Amsterdam Museum, it's a fascinating window into the 19th-century world of the super-rich, with displays including part of the family's 275-piece Meissen table service. It also has an immaculate French-style garden, and a rotating contemporary art exhibition. (amsterdammuseum.nl)

Museum Van Loon

Museum Van Loon
MUSEUM

3 MAP P84, E3

An opulent 1672 residence that was first home to painter Ferdinand Bol and later to the wealthy Van Loon family. Important paintings such as *The Marriage of Willem van Loon and Margaretha Bas* by Jan Miense Molenaer and a collection of some 150 portraits of the Van Loons hang inside sumptuous interiors. Its rear coach house once held horse-drawn carriages. In the hedged courtyard garden, the museum cafe serves lemonade and apple pie. (museumvanloon.nl)

Foam
GALLERY

4 MAP P84, E3

From the outside, it looks like a grand canal house, but these three buildings linked by staircases and passageways are the backdrop for international photographic exhibitions in spacious galleries, with an emphasis on experimentation. The Foam Editions gallery, featuring established and emerging photographers, supports the museum's educational projects. (foam.org)

Amsterdam Museum
MUSEUM

The city's history museum is temporarily being housed in the same building as H'ART (see 1 Map p84, G2) while the Amsterdam Museum's permanent home – the former City Orphanage, at Kalverstraat 92 in the Medieval Centre – undergoes renovations until 2025. This outpost's headlining exhibition,

Panorama Amsterdam, provides a chronology covering the oldest city maps, dating from 1538, to 17th-century Civic Guard portraits and contemporary street art. Temporary exhibitions take place here and at the Museum Willet-Holthuysen, also run by the Amsterdam Museum. (amsterdammuseum.nl)

Museum of the Mind | Outsider Art
MUSEUM

5 MAP P84, G2

Outside the building housing H'ART, accessed from the courtyard, the Museum of the Mind | Outsider Art was co-founded with Haarlem's Dolhuys Museum of the Mind and care organisation Cordaan. It champions artists, often with a psychological or intellectual disability, whose work is an inner expression not influenced by artistic movements or commercialism. Above the gallery, some 15 artists create in the Outsider Art Ateliers. (museum vandegeest.nl)

Leidseplein
SQUARE

6 MAP P84, A3

Historic architecture, bars, pubs, clubs, theatres and live-music venues – welcome to Leidseplein. The square, and its surrounding streets, is always busy, but after dark it's a major nightlife hub that gets thronged by a mainstream crowd of party lovers (more tourists than locals). Pavement cafes at the northern end are perfect for people-watching.

Rembrandtplein

SQUARE

7 MAP P84, E2

First called Reguliersplein, then Botermarkt for the butter markets held here until the mid-19th century, this somewhat brash square now takes its name from the cast-iron statue of the painter erected in 1876. By the early 20th century, Rembrandtplein had evolved into a nighttime hub as cafes, restaurants and clubs opened their doors, and it's still a cornerstone of Amsterdam nightlife.

Our House

MUSEUM

8 MAP P84, F2

The world's first museum of its kind, Our House showcases electronic dance music (EDM). Through its interactive installments, DJ-curated exhibitions, and immersive shows with lasers, smoke and floor-to-ceiling projections, it covers EDM's evolution from the birth of house music in Chicago warehouses, the genre's split from techno in Detroit, and illegal raves in Britain and Europe.

Symbol of Amsterdam

The city's symbol, XXX (three St Andrew's crosses), appears on its coat of arms, flag, municipal buildings and merchandising everywhere. It originated in 1505 when Amsterdam was a fishing town (St Andrew is the patron saint of fishers).

The highlight is composing your own dance piece on the metre-long sequencer. (our-house.com)

Amsterdam Pipe Museum

MUSEUM

9 MAP P84, B3

This museum is located in the grand 17th-century canal house of the marvellously single-minded pipe collector who gathered this unexpectedly fascinating collection from 60 countries over 40 years. Guided tours show the earliest South American pipes, 15th-century Dutch pipes, Chinese opium pipes, African ceremonial pipes and much more. (pipemuseum.nl)

Eating

Van Dobben

DUTCH €

10 MAP P84, E2

Open since 1945, Van Dobben has a cool diner feel, with white tiles, a marble countertop, black stools and a siren-red ceiling. Low-priced, finely sliced roast-beef sandwiches with mustard are an old-fashioned joy, or try the *pekelvlees* (akin to corned beef) or *halfom* (*pekelvlees* mixed with liver). The meat *kroketten* (croquettes) are up there with the best in town. (eetsalonvan dobben.nl)

Buffet van Odette

CAFE €€

11 MAP P84, C4

At this white-tiled cafe with an enchanting canal-side location, great ingredients and creativity come together in delicious dishes. Try the splendid platter of cured meats, or mains such as langoustine with white asparagus or pistachio-crusted lamb shoulder. (buffet-amsterdam.nl)

Zoldering

EUROPEAN €€€

12 MAP P84, F4

Michelin-starred bistro Zoldering occupies a beautiful step-gabled building dating from the 1660s, with red-brick interior walls and floor-to-ceiling windows. Refined French-Dutch cuisine incorporates seasonal market ingredients such as Waddenzee shrimp, foraged wild garlic and locally grown courgette flowers. Its extensive wine cellar has over 800 different references. (zoldering.nl)

Bakhuys Amsterdam

CAFE €

13 MAP P84, H4

In this large industrial space, watch from up close as bakers knead sourdough and work the wood-fired oven. Breakfasts such as omelettes with toast or sweet pastries are followed from noon by pizzas and filled sandwiches. Its log benches are also a great place to stop for a coffee. (bakhuys-amsterdam.nl)

De Carrousel

DUTCH €

14 MAP P84, D5

De Carrousel serves some of Amsterdam's best traditional large, thin Dutch pancakes (both sweet and savoury), as well as *poffertjes* (tiny pancakes topped with

Canal of Seven Bridges

It's easy to get swept away in the raucous local nightlife and forget that one of Amsterdam's most romantic canals flows through this neighbourhood. The **Reguliersgracht** (Map p84, E3), aka the 'canal of seven bridges', is especially enchanting by night, when its humpbacked arches glow with tiny gold lights. Though the best views are from aboard a boat, you can still get great vistas from land. In all directions it's possible to count 15 bridges.

powdered sugar) and crispy, golden waffles, but its decor also takes the cake – in the middle of the neon-lit wooden building is an old carousel (merry-go-round). A large wooden deck also provides plentiful outdoor seating. (decarrouselpannenkoeken.nl)

Klein Breda

EUROPEAN €€€

15 MAP P84, F2

Klein Breda's three- to five-course menu is always a revolving door of sustainable, regional products with little flourishes; dishes might include smoked mackerel with celeriac ice cream, or wild duck with fermented red cabbage. Exposed bulbs and white-brick walls provide a sophisticated backdrop. (bredagroup-amsterdam.com)

Embrace Gezelligheid

This particularly Dutch quality, which is most widely found in old brown cafes, is one of the best reasons to visit Amsterdam. It's variously translated as 'snug', 'friendly', 'cosy', 'informal' and 'convivial', but *gezelligheid* – the state of being *gezellig* – is more elemental. You'll feel this all-is-right-with-the-world vibe in many places and situations, often while nursing a brew with friends during *borrel* (an informal gathering over drinks). And nearly any low-lit, welcoming establishment qualifies.

Pantry

DUTCH €€

16 ✘ MAP P84, B3

With wood-panelled walls and sepia lighting, this little restaurant is *gezellig* indeed. Tuck into classic Dutch dishes such as *zuurkool stamppot* (sauerkraut and potato mash served with a smoked sausage or meatball) and *hutspot* ('hotchpotch', with stewed beef, carrots and onions). (thepantry.nl)

Petit by Sam

BAKERY €

17 ✘ MAP P84, D3

Light and bright, this little patisserie uses ingredients such as date puree, honey, and coconut and almond flours as alternatives to butter, refined sugar and white flour, making it perfect for anyone looking for a vegan, dairy-free or gluten-free pick-me-up. Sweet treats include choc-quinoa crisps, almond-flour lemon-drizzle cake and apricot and sunflower-seed slice. There's a handful of tables. (petitbysam.com)

Vegan Junk Food Bar

VEGAN €€

18 ✘ MAP P84, D2

This flashy restaurant (one of a handful around Amsterdam), with pink graffiti walls and neon lights, serves healthy 'junk' food. Plant-based burgers are wildly popular; you can also order glazed 'chicken wings' made from soy protein, BBQ ribs made from pea protein, or sashimi made from tapioca starch, along with natural wines, organic beers and fruity cocktails. (vegan junkfoodbar.com)

Piet de Leeuw

STEAK €€

19 ✘ MAP P84, D4

With its dark-wood furniture, wood-panelled walls hung with pictures, oil-painted ceiling and wrought-iron lamps, Piet de Leeuw feels like an old-school pub. The building dates from 1900, but it's been a steakhouse since 1949. Sit at individual or communal tables and tuck into good-value steaks topped with a choice of sauces and served with salad and piping-hot *frites* (French fries). (pietdeleeuw.nl)

Drinking

Flying Dutchmen Cocktails

COCKTAIL BAR

20 MAP P84, C1

Amsterdam's best cocktail bar inspires awe even among connoisseurs. Within 1662 national monument the Odeon, this award-winning venture by renowned mixologists Timo Janse and Tess Posthumus is a spectacular setting for the Netherlands' largest backbar, with over 800 different spirits. Reserve online to learn the craft during cocktail workshops. (flyingdutchmencocktails.shop)

Back to Black

CAFE

21 MAP P84, C4

It's easy to lose track of time in this ultra-cool neighbourhood cafe with teal walls, exposed light bulbs and wood shelves hanging on ropes. Back to Black chooses its beans with care and roasts them locally in Amsterdam. It also serves a small but stellar selection of cakes and pastries. (backtoblackcoffee.nl)

Door 74

COCKTAIL BAR

22 MAP P84, E2

It's best to book seats online or by phone to gain entry to this speakeasy behind an unmarked door (or try ringing the doorbell). Innovative cocktails are served in a classy, dark-timbered Prohibition-era atmosphere beneath pressed-tin ceilings. (finddoor74.com)

Shiraz Jardin des Vins

WINE BAR

23 MAP P84, B4

There are no reservations at this contemporary wine bar; drop in for over 260 different old- and new-world wines expertly selected by sommeliers, and accompanied by charcuterie and cheese platters. In warm weather, the best seats are on the canal-side terrace or its canal boat. You can also buy bottles at the shop. (shirazamsterdam.nl)

Coco's Corner Shop

JUICE BAR

24 MAP P84, E2

Revitalise with organic juices, power smoothies, shots such as wheatgrass or ginger, and homemade lemonades at this small shop, with mezzanine seating above. It's also

Vegan Junk Food Bar

GRUVI BLUM/SHUTTERSTOCK ©

Southern Canal Ring Drinking

great for old-fashioned milkshakes, iced coffees, and lattes like pink beetroot and almond milk, dragon fruit and coconut milk, or CBD oil and matcha. (cocoscornershop-amsterdam.nl)

Bocca Coffee COFFEE

25 🚃 MAP P84, C3

The team behind Bocca Coffee knows its stuff, sourcing beans from Ethiopia to sell to cafes across the city since 2001. It's now serving some seriously good caffeine in this light, spacious coffeehouse. Perch at the wooden bar or get comfy in a vintage armchair, or sign up for courses including coffee art, tasting and brewing, or espresso at home. (bocca.nl)

Secret Garden COCKTAIL BAR

26 🚃 MAP P84, D2

Stepping inside the Secret Garden transports you to a lush tropical rainforest thanks to its botanical and bird murals, hanging plants and wrought-iron seating in a vine-draped courtyard. Equally exotic are cocktails like pisco and purple-corn liqueur sour, or mezcal, honey and grapefruit foam, and Asian and Peruvian-influenced dishes (eg king crab and prawn toast, or yellowtail ceviche with yuzu). (secretgarden amsterdam.com)

Café Brecht BAR

27 🚃 MAP P84, C5

Café Brecht is one of Amsterdam's loveliest bars, with mismatched armchairs, vintage furniture, books and board games; all are a hit with a young and gorgeously boho crowd – it gets absolutely crammed in here. It's named after seminal German dramatist and poet Bertolt Brecht, hence the German poetry inscribed on the walls, and the all-German beer and wine. (cafebrecht.nl)

LGBTIQ+ Venues in the Southern Canal Ring

The Southern Canal Ring is home to numerous LGBTIQ+ venues, especially on rainbow-flag-adorned Reguliersdwarsstraat, as well as Kerkstraat and Rembrandtplein.

Popular **Taboo Bar** (Map p84, D2; taboobar.nl) has drag shows, DJs, happy hours and patrons spilling out into the street. **Blend XL** (Map p84, D2; barblend.nl), with numerous rooms and disco-ball-lit dance floor, adjoins lesbian bar **B'Femme** (Map p84, D2; instagram.com/bfemme), with an intimate dance area. **Club NYX** (Map p84, D2; clubnyx.nl) has three floors, each with a different style of music. Singalongs and quiz nights are part of the fun at **Montmartre** (Map p84, E2; cafemontmartre.nl). A super-hot crowd makes their way to cruise club **Church** (Map p84, B3; clubchurch.nl).

Oosterling BROWN CAFE

28 MAP P84, F4

Opened in 1735 as a tea and coffee outlet for the Dutch East India Company, Oosterling is now run by friendly brothers Oscar and Marcel, the fourth generation of Oosterlings at the helm since 1877. It's one of the very few *cafés* with an off-licence bottle-shop permit. (cafeoosterling.nl)

Entertainment

Koninklijk Theater Tuschinski CINEMA

29 MAP P84, E2

This fantastical 1921-completed, 1431-capacity cinema, a prime example of the Amsterdam School of architecture, is worth visiting for its sumptuous art-deco interior alone. The *grote zaal* (main auditorium) is the most stunning; it generally screens blockbusters, while the smaller theatres play arthouse and indie films. Morning tours of the interiors lasting 45 minutes take place before screenings. (pathe.nl)

Melkweg LIVE MUSIC

30 MAP P84, A3

In a former dairy, the nonprofit 'Milky Way' offers a dazzling diversity of gigs, featuring both DJs and live bands, from 'Techno Tuesday', to reggae, punk and heavy metal. Roots, folk and rock also get stage time. Check out the website for cinema, theatre and multimedia offerings, too. (melkweg.nl)

Paradiso LIVE MUSIC

31 MAP P84, B4

In 1968, a beautiful old church turned into the 'Cosmic Relaxation Center Paradiso'. Today, the vibe is less hippy than funky odyssey, with big all-nighters, themed events and indie nights. The smaller hall hosts up-and-coming bands, and in the Main Hall it seems the stained-glass windows might shatter under the force of the beats. (paradiso.nl)

Bourbon Street Jazz & Blues Club LIVE MUSIC

32 MAP P84, B3

This intimate venue has a full and eclectic music programme. Check the website for a list of open jam sessions and performances ranging from jazz, blues and soul to rock, Latin and pop. (bourbonstreet.nl)

Jazz Café Alto JAZZ

33 MAP P84, B3

Here since 1953, this is an intimate, atmospheric *bruin café*–style locations for serious jazz and (occasionally) blues. There are live gigs nightly – it doesn't take reservations so arrive early if you want to snag a seat. Jam sessions are free. (jazz-cafe-alto.nl)

Koninklijk Theater Carré PERFORMING ARTS

34 MAP P84, H4

The Carré family started their career with a horse act at the annual fair, progressing to this circus theatre in 1887. The faces of jesters, dancers and theatre folk adorn the classical facade. With a capacity of 1700, it hosts a great programme of quality music and theatre; the Christmas circus is a seasonal highlight. There's a top-floor Dutch restaurant. (carre.nl)

De Uitkijk
CINEMA

35 ⭐ MAP P84, B3

Opened in 1912 in a 17th-century warehouse on the Prinsengracht, this arthouse stalwart is the city's oldest surviving cinema and has a an eclectic movie menu that mixes classic oldies with more recent and foreign films in their original languages (including English). (uitkijk.nl)

Dutch Design 🖊

Contemporary Dutch design has a reputation for minimalist, creative approaches to everyday furniture and homewares, mixed with vintage twists and tongue-in-cheek humour to keep it fresh. What started out as a few innovators accelerated to become a movement that put the Netherlands at the forefront of the industry. Dutch fashion is also reaching far beyond the country's borders, with designs that are vibrant and imaginative, yet practical.

Shopping

Moooi
DESIGN

36 🔒 MAP P84, F4

Founded by Dutch designers Marcel Wanders and Casper Vissers, this gallery-shop features Dutch design at its most over-the-top, for instance a spun fibreglass chandelier, carbon-fibre chair, modular 'BFF sofa', life-size black horse lamp, or 'blow away vase' (a whimsical twist on the classic Delft vase). (moooi.com)

Concerto
MUSIC

37 🔒 MAP P84, F3

Established in 1955 and rambling over five floors, the Netherlands' largest music shop is muso heaven, with a fabulous selection of new and secondhand vinyl and CDs encompassing every imaginable genre, including rockabilly, classical and more. It's good value and has listening facilities, plus a sofa-strewn, living-room-style cafe and regular live sessions. (concerto.nl)

Kramer Kunst & Antiek
ANTIQUES

38 🔒 MAP P84, C3

Specialising in antique blue-and-white Dutch tiles, this engrossing, crammed-to-the-rafters shop is chock-a-block with fascinating antiques, silver candlesticks, crystal decanters, jewellery and pocket watches. It's now run by the third generation of Kramers, brothers Sebastian and Eduard. (antique-tileshop.nl)

Vlieger STATIONERY

39 MAP P84, E2

Love stationery and paper? Make a beeline for Vlieger. Since 1869, this two-storey shop has been supplying it all: Egyptian papyrus, beautiful handmade papers from Asia and Central America, papers inlaid with flower petals or bamboo, and paper textured like snakeskin. (vliegerpapier.nl)

Shirt Shop CLOTHING

40 MAP P84, D2

On Amsterdam's main gay street, this shop has a kaleidoscopic array of the go-to going-out garb for many locals: smart shirts with cool geometric and abstract designs as well as tulip, windmill, animals and bird motifs, plus T-shirts and sweaters. All are handpicked from European collections. (shirtshop amsterdam.com)

Rain Couture FASHION & ACCESSORIES

41 MAP P84, F4

Even if it rains, you can stay dry and stylish with outerwear and accessories made from breathable, waterproof smart fabrics by local designer Daphne Gerritse. There are many styles such as trench coats, three-in-ones, ponchos and parkas. (rain-couture.nl)

Spiegel DESIGN

42 MAP P84, D2

For 100% Dutch-designed gifts, head to this light-filled boutique with tantalising jewellery, bags, hats, art and tableware from

Utrechtsestraat

A stone's throw south from gaudy Rembrandtplein, Utrechtsestraat is stocked with enticing shops, designer bars and cosy eateries – a prime place to wander and discover a great local hangout. The street's southern end used to terminate at the Utrechtse Poort, a gate to the nearby city of Utrecht, hence the name.

creators including Kitsch Kitchen, Het Muizenhuis, Mariska Meijers and Cre8. Most items will fit in your suitcase but it also ships worldwide. (spiegelamsterdam.nl)

Property Of... DESIGN

43 MAP P84, F2

This Amsterdam-based label produces dapper travel gear, from backpacks to tote bags, using chrome-free leather and recycled materials. (thepropertyof.com)

Skateboards Amsterdam SPORTS & OUTDOORS

44 MAP P84, D3

Skater-dude heaven, with everything required for the freewheeling lifestyle: cruisers, longboards, shortboards, electric and off-road boards, along with shoes, laces, caps, beanies, bags, backpacks, and clothing including Spitfire and Thrasher T-shirts and a fantastic selection of band T-shirts. (skate boardsamsterdam.nl)

Explore
Vondelpark & the South

Museumplein, in the south of the city, is home to the Rijksmuseum, Van Gogh and Stedelijk museums. Nearby, Vondelpark has a special place in Amsterdam's heart; a lush, green, egalitarian space where everyone ends up at some point: cyclists, picnickers and sunbathers. In the north, you'll find cultural centre De Hallen and hip Overtoom, crammed with cafes, restaurants and bars.

The Short List

○ **Rijksmuseum (p98)** *Getting happily lost amid the riches of one of the world's finest museums.*

○ **Van Gogh Museum (p102)** *Seeing the world's best collection of Van Gogh's work up close, from vibrant yellow sunflowers to purple-blue irises.*

○ **Vondelpark (p106)** *Freewheeling through the city's green heart.*

○ **Stedelijk Museum (p109)** *Discovering works by Matisse, Warhol, Yayoi Kusama and more at Amsterdam's fabulous modern-art museum.*

○ **De Hallen (p116)** *Dining at the food hall inside this cultural centre in repurposed tram sheds.*

Getting There & Around

🚊 Trams 2, 3, 5 and 12 stop at Museumplein, near the Vondelpark's main entrance. The Vondelpark's southern side is served by tram 2. The northern side, along Overtoom, is served by trams 1 and 17. Trams 7 and 17 travel along Kinkerstraat.

Neighbourhood Map on p108

Museumplein (p110) PANDORA PICTURES/SHUTTERSTOCK ©

Top Experience

Admire art at the Rijksmuseum

The Rijksmuseum is a magnificent repository of art and it's the only museum with a cycle lane through its centre. Beautifully presented, it includes masterpieces by homegrown geniuses such as Rembrandt, Vermeer and Van Gogh. It was conceived to hold several national and royal collections, which occupy 1.5km of gallery space.

🎯 MAP P108, E2

National Museum
rijksmuseum.nl

Floor 2: 1600–1700

Start your visit on the 2nd floor, which contains the highlights of the collection, with its Golden Age masterpieces, in the **Gallery of Honour**. It's a bit convoluted to reach, but well-signposted.

Frans Hals

Frans Hals painted with broad brushstrokes and a fluidity that was unique for his time. *The Merry Drinker* (1628–30) shows his style in action. No one knows who the gent with the beer glass is, but it's clear he's enjoying himself after a hard day of work.

Johannes (Jan) Vermeer

This floor hosts beautiful works by Vermeer, with intimate domestic scenes rendered in almost photographic detail. Check out the dreamy *Milkmaid* (1660; also called *The Kitchen Maid*). Notice the holes in the wall? The shadow under the nail? In *Woman in Blue Reading a Letter* (1663), Vermeer shows only parts of the table, chairs, map and other objects, leaving the viewer to figure out the rest.

Jan Steen

Jan Steen became renowned for painting chaotic households to convey moral teachings, as in *The Merry Family* (1668). None of the drunken adults notice the little boy sneaking a taste of wine. In the 18th century the expression 'a Jan Steen household' entered the local lexicon to mean a crazy state of affairs.

Rembrandt

You'll find several wonderful works by Rembrandt, including his resigned, unflinching self-portrait as the Apostle Paul. *The Jewish Bride* (1665), showing a couple's intimate caress, impressed Van Gogh so much that he declared

Vondelpark & the South Rijksmuseum

★ **Top Tips**

o Friday, Saturday and Sunday are the busiest days. It's least crowded before 10am and after 3pm.

o Buy tickets and choose entry times online; you need to reserve a timeslot in advance even if you already have a ticket or museum pass.

o Download the museum's free app. It has a self-guided tour, or you can select works by number.

o While you can see the highlights in a couple of hours, the collection is huge so consider allowing much longer.

✗ **Take a Break**

Treat yourself to a gourmet lunch or dinner at **Rijks** (rijksrestaurant.nl), the Michelin-starred museum restaurant.

For something less formal, there's a **cafe** on the mezzanine in the great entrance atrium and one out in the garden during summer.

Rijksmuseum

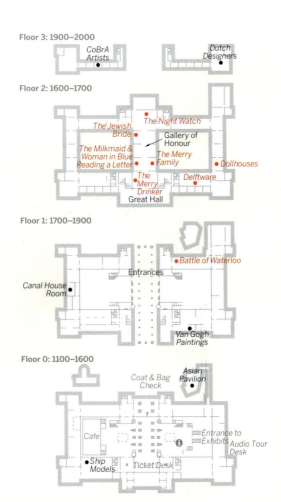

Floor 3: 1900–2000

CoBrA Artists

Dutch Designers

Floor 2: 1600–1700

The Night Watch

The Jewish Bride

Gallery of Honour

The Milkmaid & Woman in Blue Reading a Letter

The Merry Family

Dollhouses

The Merry Drinker

Delftware

Great Hall

Floor 1: 1700–1900

Battle of Waterloo

Entrances

Canal House Room

Van Gogh Paintings

Floor 0: 1100–1600

Coat & Bag Check

Asian Pavilion

Cafe

Entrance to Exhibits

Audio Tour Desk

Ship Models

Ticket Desk

he would give up a decade of his life just to sit before the painting for a fortnight with only a crust of bread to eat.

The Night Watch

Rembrandt's gigantic *The Night Watch* (1642) is the rock star of the Rijksmuseum, with perennial crowds in front of it. The work's original title is *Archers under the Command of Captain Frans Banning Cocq,* and *The Night Watch* name was bestowed years later, thanks to a layer of grime that gave the impression it was a nocturnal scene. It has since been restored to its original colours.

Delftware

Intriguing Golden Age swag fills the rooms on either side of the Gallery of Honour. Delftware was the Dutch attempt to reproduce Chinese porcelain in the late 1600s; Gallery 2.22 displays lots of the delicate blue-and-white pottery.

Dollhouses

Gallery 2.20 is devoted to mind-blowing dollhouses. Merchant's wife Petronella Oortman employed carpenters, glassblowers and silversmiths to make the 700 items inside her dollhouse, using the same materials as they would for full-scale versions.

Floor 3: 1900–2000

The uppermost floor has a limited, but interesting, collection.

It includes avant-garde, childlike paintings by Karel Appel, Constant Nieuwenhuys and their compadres in the post-WWII CoBrA movement, and cool furnishings by Dutch designers such as Gerrit Rietveld and Michel de Klerk.

Floor 1: 1700–1900

Highlights on Floor 1 include the *Battle of Waterloo,* the Rijksmuseum's largest painting, taking up almost an entire wall in Gallery 1.12. Three Van Gogh paintings hang in Gallery 1.18. Gallery 1.16 re-creates a gilded, 18th-century canal-house room.

Floor 0: 1100–1600

This floor is packed with fascinating curiosities. The **Special Collections** have sections including magic lanterns, an armoury, ship models and silver miniatures. The serene **Asian Pavilion**, a separate structure that's often free from crowds, holds first-rate artworks from China, Indonesia, Japan, India, Thailand and Vietnam.

Facade & Gardens

Pierre Cuypers designed the 1885 building. Check out the exterior, which mixes neo-Gothic and Dutch Renaissance styles. The museum's gardens – aka the 'outdoor gallery' – host big-name sculpture exhibitions at least once a year. You can stroll for free amid the roses, hedges, fountains and a cool greenhouse.

Top Experience 📷

See the work of a master at the Van Gogh Museum

Trace Van Gogh's tragic yet breathtakingly productive life at this wonderful museum holding the world's largest collection of his work. Opened in 1973 to house the collection of his younger brother Theo, the museum comprises some 200 paintings and 500 drawings by Vincent and his contemporaries, including Gauguin and Monet.

🎯 MAP P108, E3

vangoghmuseum.nl

Museum Layout

The museum spreads over four levels, moving chronologically from Floor 0 (aka the ground floor) to Floor 3. Many of Van Gogh's most famous works are on floors 0 and 1, but sometimes works are moved, so check the website or the guides when you get there if there's something you don't want to miss.

In all, the museum is a manageable size; allow a couple of hours or so to browse the galleries (longer if you're a dedicated fan).

The Potato Eaters

Van Gogh's earliest works – showing raw, if unrefined, talent – are from his time in the Dutch countryside and in Antwerp between 1883 and 1885. He painted peasant life, exalting their existence in such works as *The Potato Eaters* (1885).

Bible & Skeleton

The symbolic *Still Life with Bible* (1885), painted after his father's death, shows a burnt-out candle, his Protestant minister father's bible, and a much-thumbed smaller book, *La Joie de Vivre*, representing Van Gogh's more secular philosophy. *Skeleton with Burning Cigarette* (1886) – the print all the stoners are buying in the gift shop – was painted when Van Gogh was a student at Antwerp's Royal Academy of Fine Arts.

Self-Portraits

In 1886 Van Gogh moved to Paris, where his brother Theo was working as an art dealer. Vincent began to paint multiple self-portraits as a way of improving his portraiture without paying for models, which he was too poor to afford. He met some of the Impressionists, and his palette began to brighten.

★ **Top Tips**

o Tickets must be pre-purchased online with a set time slot – including for museum pass holders. Tickets sell out days in advance.

o Arrive before 11am or after 3pm, or visit late on Friday in summer to avoid the crowds.

o Ask about workshops and activities such as treasure hunts for kids during holiday periods.

✗ **Take a Break**

There's a museum **cafe** serving soups, sandwiches and light dishes.

Steps away on Paulus Potterstraat, *Wizard of Oz*–themed restaurant/bar the **Burger Room** (p112) has fantastic burgers.

Van Gogh Museum

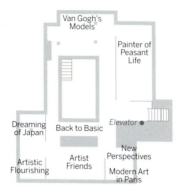

Van Gogh's Models

Painter of Peasant Life

Dreaming of Japan

Back to Basic

Elevator

Artistic Flourishing

Artist Friends

New Perspectives

Modern Art in Paris

Floor 1

Cafe

Self-Portraits

Timeline

Workshops

Paulus Potterstraat

Group Entrance

Elevator

To Main Entrance & Exhibition Wing

Shop

Floor 0

Sunflowers

In 1888 Van Gogh left for Arles in Provence to paint its colourful landscapes. Paintings of *Sunflowers* (1889) and other blossoms that shimmer with intense Mediterranean light are from this period.

The Yellow House & Bedroom

Other paintings from his time in Arles include *The Yellow House* (1888), a rendering of the abode Van Gogh rented in town, intending to start an artists' colony with Gauguin. *The Bedroom* (1888) depicts Van Gogh's sleeping quarters at the house (the walls were originally purple but as the red pigment has faded, they now appear blue instead).

It was in this house in 1888 that Van Gogh sliced off part of his ear.

Wheatfield with Crows

Van Gogh had himself committed to an asylum in St-Rémy in 1889. While there, he painted several landscapes with cypress and olive trees, and went wild with a famous rendition of *Irises* in 1890. That year he went north to Auvers-sur-Oise. *Wheatfield with Crows* (1890), one of his last paintings, is an ominous work finished shortly before his suicide.

Vincent's Letters

The museum has multiple listening stations for diverse recordings of Van Gogh's letters, mainly to and from his closest brother, Theo, who championed his work.

The museum has categorised all of Van Gogh's letters online at vangoghletters.org.

Other Artists

Thanks to Theo van Gogh's prescient collecting and that of the museum's curators, you'll also see works by Vincent's contemporaries, including Gauguin, Monet and Henri de Toulouse-Lautrec.

Exhibition Wing

Gerrit Rietveld, the influential Dutch architect, designed the museum's main building. Behind it, reaching towards the Museumplein, is a separate wing (opened in 1999) designed by Kisho Kurokawa and commonly referred to as 'the Mussel'. It hosts temporary exhibitions by big-name artists.

Top Experience 📷

Wander through Vondelpark

Vondelpark is Amsterdam's beloved green jewel. On a sunny day, you'll see cyclists and in-line skaters flying past parents with prams and picnickers. A mixture of manicured gardens and shady greenery spans a whopping 47 hectares (116 acres). Vondelpark receives over 10 million visitors annually, and hosts plenty of outdoor events – it's rarely tranquil, but always good fun.

◎ MAP P108, E2

hetvondelpark.net

Vondel Statue

The English-style gardens, with ponds, lawns, footbridges and winding footpaths, were laid out in 1865 and originally known as Nieuwe Park (New Park). In 1867, sculptor Louis Royer added a **statue** of famed poet and playwright Joost van den Vondel (1587–1679). Amsterdammers began referring to the place as Vondel's Park, which led to it being renamed.

Hippie Legacies

During the late 1960s and early 1970s, Dutch authorities turned the park into a temporary open-air dormitory for the droves of hippies who descended on Amsterdam. The sleeping bags are long gone, but remnants of the era live on in the squats that fringe the park, such as **OT301** (ot301.nl) and **OCCII** (occii.org), now both legalised into underground cultural centres.

Gardens & Grounds

The park's 47 hectares encourage visitors to get out and explore. The **rose garden**, with some 70 species, was added in 1936. It's in the middle of the park; signs point the way. The park also contains several cafes, playgrounds and a summertime outdoor **theatre** (openluchttheater.nl).

Picasso Sculpture

Art is strewn throughout the park, with 69 sculptures dotted throughout the leafy environs. Among them is Picasso's soaring abstract **work** *Figure découpée l'Oiseau (The Bird),* better known locally as *The Fish* (1965), which he donated for the park's centenary.

★ Top Tips

o It's great to glide around and explore the park by bike. Take yours there or hire one nearby.

o Sunday is fun day at Vondelpark, when there's almost a festival atmosphere on sunny days.

o Look out for events at the park's open-air theatre during summer.

✕ Take a Break

The elegant cake-stand architecture of **Proeflokaal 't Blauwe Theehuis** (brouwerijhetij.nl) makes for an excellent spot to sip Brouwerij 't IJ craft beer on its inviting terrace.

Like a secret garden-within-a-garden, family-friendly cafe **Vondeltuin** (devondeltuin.nl) comes into its own in summer with outdoor picnic-style tables amid the greenery.

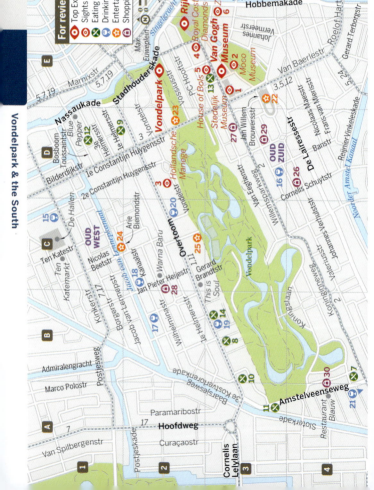

For reviews see

Top Experiences		p98
Sights		p109
Eating		p110
Drinking		p112
Entertainment		p114
Shopping		p116

200 m
0.1 miles

Rijksmuseum

Royal Coster Diamonds

Zuiderbad

Van Gogh Museum 6

Hobbemakade

Boerenweetering

Johannes Vermeer

Moco Museum

Van Baerlestr

House of Bols

Stedelijk Museum

Jan Willem Brouwersstr

De Lairessestr

OUD ZUID

Cornelis Schuytstr

Vondelpark

Stadhouderskade

Nassaukade

Bosboom Toussaintstr

Blue Pepper

Bilderdijkstr

1e Constantijn Huygenstr

2e Constantijn Huygenstr

Hollandsche Manege

De Hallen

Ten Katestr

Ten Katemarkt

OUD WEST

Nicolaas Beetsstr

Arie Biemondstr

Kinkerstr

Borgerstr

Jacob van Lennepstr

Jacob van Lennepkanaal

Jan Pieter Heijestr

Warna Baru

Wilhelminastr

1e Helmersstr

Overtoom

This is Soul

Gerard Brandtstr

Vondelstr

Vondelkerkstr

Admiralengracht

Postjesweg

Marco Polostr

Baarsjesweg

2e Kostverlorenkade

Paramaribostr

Hoofdweg

Curaçaostr

Van Spilbergenstr

Postjeskade

Cornelis Lelylaan

Amstelveenseweg

Restaurant Blauw

Sloterkade

Koninginneweg

Koningslaan

Valeriusstr

Johannes Verhulststr

Reijnier Vinkeleskade

Nicolaas Maesstr

Frans van Mierisstr

Banstr

Roelof Hartstr

Gerard Terborgstr

Ferdinand Bolstr

Frans Halsstr

De Pijp

1e Jan Steenstr

Noorder Amstel Kanaal

Van Eeghenstr

Willemsparkweg

PC Hooftstr

Vossiusstr

Max Euweplein

Singelgracht

Marnixstr

Sights

Stedelijk Museum   MUSEUM

1 ◉ MAP P108, E3

This fabulous museum houses the collection amassed by postwar curator Willem Sandberg. A rotating selection of highlights from its 90,000-strong collection of modern and contemporary visual art and design from 1870 to the present day features artists including Picasso, Matisse, Mondrian, Van Gogh, Rothko, Jeff Koons, Yves Klein, Lichtenstein and Yayoi Kusama. The free audio-guide is fantastic; the museum also hosts excellent temporary exhibitions. AM Weissman's Dutch Renaissance–style main building dates from 1895; the 2012 extension is fittingly nicknamed 'the Bathtub'. (stedelijk.nl)

Moco Museum   MUSEUM

2 ◉ MAP P108, E3

Overlooking Museumplein, a beautiful private house, the 1904 Villa Alsberg, has been converted into the independent 'Modern Contemporary' (Moco) museum by private collectors and curators Lionel and Kim Logchies. Its collection includes modern, contemporary and street art by artists including Andy Warhol, Keith Haring, Damien Hirst and Banksy. Sculptures displayed in the garden include a giant red gummy bear by artist WhIsBe and outsized rocking horse by Dutch designer Marcel Wanders. Temporary exhibitions take place throughout the year. (mocomuseum.com)

Hollandsche Manege   MUSEUM

3 ◉ MAP P108, D2

Entering the neoclassical Hollandsche Manege is like stepping back in time into a grandiose indoor riding school inspired by Vienna's famous Spanish Riding School. Designed by AL van Gendt and built in 1882, it retains its charming horsehead facade. Its Levend Paarden Museum (Living Horse Museum) details the building's history alongside the 'world of the horse' through equine art and displays including historic riding equipment. Visitors can book in advance for 30-minute or hour-long private riding lessons at its arena. (dehollandschemanege.nl)

Royal Coster Diamonds   FACTORY

4 ◉ MAP P108, E2

Founded in 1840, Royal Coster is the world's oldest working diamond factory. On free guided tours, you can watch craftspeople cut and polish rough stones into sparkling gems, while learning about the origins of diamonds and assessing their quality and value. Also here is the world's largest collection of unset diamonds and the Royal 201 diamond, glittering with 201 facets. The company also runs the neighbouring **Diamond Museum** (diamondmuseum.com), which delves into the history of diamonds in Amsterdam. (royalcoster.com)

Open-Air Cultural Space

Amsterdam's most famous museums cluster around **Museumplein**. The vast, public square was first laid out for an 1883 world fair, gaining its lasting title when the Rijksmuseum opened two years later.

Locals and tourists mill around Museumplein's grassy expanse. A children's playground occupies the northeastern corner, and an ice-skating pond typically sets up in winter. Everyone picnics here when the weather warms up: there's a large Albert Heijn supermarket beneath the southwestern corner, and food and craft stalls at the **Museum Market** (museummarket.nl) on the third Sunday of the month. Public concerts and events regularly take place throughout the year.

House of Bols
MUSEUM

5 · MAP P108, E3

Cheesy but fun: here you undertake an hour's self-guided tour through this *jenever* (Dutch gin) museum. In the 'Hall of Taste' you'll try to differentiate between scents and flavours, while in the 'Distillery Room' you'll discover the process of extraction. You'll learn more about the history of gin than you would think possible, get to try shaking your own cocktail, and drink a Bols concoction of your choice at the end. All visitors must be 18 or older. (bols.com)

Zuiderbad
SWIMMING

6 · MAP P108, F3

Originally the Velox cycling school, dating from 1897, this building behind the Rijksmuseum was converted into a splendid public pool. It's a grand 1912 edifice restored to its original glory, full of tiles, wooden changerooms and appreciative paddlers. There are steam cabins and herbal baths. The schedule for swimming (*recreatiezwemmen in diep water*) varies daily; check it online. (amsterdam.nl/zuiderbad)

Eating

Ron Gastrobar
INTERNATIONAL €€€

7 · MAP P108, B4

Ron Blaauw ran his two-Michelin-star restaurant in these pared-down, spacious designer premises before turning it into a casual fine-dining 'gastrobar' (still Michelin-starred), where you get the quality with just a dash of formality. Gourmet tapas-style dishes, dry-aged rib steaks and stellar seafood as well as excellent vegetarian dishes are served for sharing. Reservations are a must. (rongastrobar.nl)

Focacceria
ITALIAN €

8 · MAP P108, B3

Ultra-soft Genoa-style focaccia is the speciality of this tiny shop run by Italian owners Valeria and Marco. In their zero-waste kitchen, handmade focaccia is topped with fresh ingredients such as home-made pesto and Dutch cheese or whatever's in season, be it zucchini blossoms or crushed tomatoes. Focacceria is open from Wednesday to Sunday until 5pm or until the day's fare sells out.

Hap Hmm

DUTCH €€

9  MAP P108, D1

With old family photos adorning the walls, an evening at this cosy eatery almost feels like dining in someone's home. The menu offers an array of classic Dutch comfort foods, from grandmother's recipe meatballs to rich beef stew and chicken casserole, as well as schnitzel considered Amsterdam's best, all served with a selection of boiled vegetables. (hap-hmm.nl)

Adam

GASTRONOMY €€€

10 MAP P108, B3

This seriously gourmet, chic and intimate restaurant serves exquisitely presented food. Four, five or six-course surprise menus (vegetarian or meat and fish dishes) change every two months and are unfailingly delicious, with standouts like white asparagus with black-pepper crumble or venison with spiced-pear foam. Paired wines are available. (restaurantadam.nl)

Braai BBQ Bar

BARBECUE €€

11 MAP P108, A3

Once a *haringhuis* (herring stand), this tiny place is now a street-food-style barbecue bar, with a great canal-side setting. Braai's speciality is marinated, barbecued ribs (half

Museum Market

or full rack), *biltong* (a type of dried meat from South Africa) and sausages. Big sharing plates can be enjoyed at tables scattered under the trees by the water. (braaiamster dam.nl)

SottoZero

GELATO €

12 ✖️ MAP P108, D1

Homemade gelato at this little boutique is served in cups, or homemade cinnamon or dark-chocolate waffle cones. Its changing array of flavours (with 18 choices on any given day) might include creamy options like Ricotta Stregata with hazelnuts and orange zest, or Cioccolato All'Azteca with chilli, chocolate and spices, and fruit-based Tarocco (blood orange) or Cocomero (watermelon).

Burger Room

BURGERS €€

13 ✖️ MAP P108, E3

A *Wizard of Oz* theme gives this restaurant/bar an enchanted quality. Its emerald-hued decor and photos recall the 1939 film, as do burgers such as If I Only Had a Heart (beef patty topped with tortilla chips, chilli con carne and guacamole), Scarecrow (double beef, bacon and cheese) or the Twister (with a half-lobster thermidor on the side) and cocktails. (theburgerroom.com)

Alchemist Garden

VEGAN €

14 ✖️ MAP P108, B3

This bright, high-ceilinged cafe's vegan menu is gluten- and sugar-free – and very tasty. There's a health-rich, superfood-spiked organic menu with dishes such as raw 'hot dog', pumpkin burger and pesto-stuffed portobello mushrooms, plus smoothies, juices, a huge range of herbal teas and organic wine by the bottle. Many ingredients are from the owner's garden. (facebook.com/alchemistgarden)

Drinking

Lot61

COFFEE

15 ☕ MAP P108, C1

Look downstairs to the open cellar to see (and, better still, smell) fresh coffee beans being roasted on the Probat at this streetwise spot. Beans are sourced through distributors from individual ecofriendly farms in Brazil, Kenya and Rwanda, to name a few. All coffees are double shots (unless you specify otherwise); watch Kinkerstraat's passing parade from a window seat. (lot61.com)

Lillie Wine Rebel

WINE BAR

16 ☕ MAP P108, D3

Set over two levels with a street-side summer terrace, this wine bar serves selections from the 'cradle of wine' – Austria, Georgia, Greece, Hungary, Lebanon and Romania. Over 50 are available at any one time. Along with charcuterie and cheese platters, small sharing plates include blini with salmon and trout caviar, burrata with grilled asparagus or brioche with duck rillettes. (lilliewinerebel.nl)

Indonesian Cuisine

Due to the Netherlands' colonial history in Indonesia, several generations of Indonesians have settled here. As such, Amsterdam has plenty of places to try the island nation's cuisine.

The most popular Indonesian dish here is a *rijsttafel* (literally 'rice table', or known as an Indonesian banquet): a dozen or more tiny dishes such as braised beef, pork satay and ribs served with white rice. Other popular dishes are *nasi goreng* – fried rice with onion, pork, shrimp and spices, often topped with a fried egg or shredded omelette – and *bami goreng*, which is the same thing but with noodles in place of rice. Indonesian food is usually served mild for Western palates. If you want it hot (*pedis*, pronounced 'p-dis'), say so, but be prepared for the ride of a lifetime.

Top Indonesian dining addresses near Vondelpark include **Restaurant Blauw** (Map p108, A4; restaurantblauw.nl), which offers meat, seafood or vegetarian *rijsttafel* feasts; **Blue Pepper** (Map p108, D1; restaurantbluepepper.com), one of Amsterdam's finest gourmet Indonesian restaurants; and fresh, contemporary **Warna Baru** (Map p108, C2; warnabaru.nl), with floral-patterned sofas, bright yellow and blue walls, and vibrant dishes such as jackfruit rendang (stew), eggs in Balinese sauce and coconut-fried banana, designed to share. Fiery cocktails include Gunung Merapi (pandan rum, chilli liqueur and lychee juice).

Staring at Jacob

CAFE

17 MAP P108, B2

Named for the canal its sunny terrace overlooks, this buzzing cafe has fantastic dirty Bloody Marys (five different kinds, including the Dirty Dirty, with pickle juice, bacon and chilli), an extensive gin collection, homemade seltzers and lemonades, Amsterdam-brewed beers, boozy hot chocolates and rich milkshakes served in mason jars. Book ahead for lavish brunches. (staringatjacob.nl)

Gebrouwen door Vrouwen

MICROBREWERY

18 MAP P108, C2

Sisters Tessel and Do de Hey began brewing as a hobby that morphed into their own microbrewery, where you can sample unique brews such as Zonnig Zeewit (North Sea seaweed white ale), Pumpkin Party (cinnamon and nutmeg pumpkin ale) or Gember Goud (ginger pale ale) at the golden-tiled bar. (gebrouwendoorvrouwen.nl)

Craft & Draft
CRAFT BEER

19 MAP P108, B3

Craft-beer fans are spoilt for choice, with no fewer than 40 beers from around the world rotating on the taps and 60 more by the bottle. Try house collaborations with Netherlands brewers such as the Big Fat 5 Double IPA with five different hop varieties or Dutch Eagle American Pale Ale. The outdoor terrace gets busy in summer. (craftanddraft.nl)

Plan B
BAR

20 MAP P108, C2

If your Vondelpark football game's washed out, switch to Plan B. This friendly pool hall offers dartboards, table tennis and a wall of board games – all first come, first served. There's craft beer on tap. (planbovertoom.nl)

Butcher's Tears
BREWERY

21 MAP P108, A4

In-the-know hop heads like to go straight to the source of cult brewers Butcher's Tears. The brewery's all-white, clinical-feeling taproom is tucked at the end of an out-of-the-way industrial alley and offers a rotating line-up of beers on tap, drawing inspiration from historical brewing techniques. You can pull up a chair in the front car park on sunny days. (butchers-tears.com)

Entertainment

Concertgebouw
CLASSICAL MUSIC

22 MAP P108, E3

The Concert Hall was built in 1888 by AL van Gendt, who engineered its near-perfect acoustics. Bernard Haitink, former conductor of the Royal Concertgebouw Orchestra, remarked that the world-famous hall was the orchestra's best instrument. Free half-hour concerts take place Wednesdays at 12.30pm from September to June; arrive early. Substantially discounted concerts are held from 11am to noon on Sundays. (concertgebouw.nl)

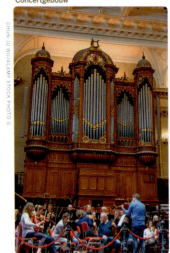

Concertgebouw

Worth a Trip:
Amsterdamse Bos

South of the urban idyll of Vondelpark, you can get a true taste of the countryside on the city's fringe. First planted from 1934 to provide employment during the Great Depression, **Amsterdamse Bos** (Amsterdam Forest; amsterdamsebos.nl) sprawls over some 1000 hectares of woodland, meadows and waterways, with squirrels, frogs, salamanders and abundant birdlife, including waterfowl.

Forest Adventures

By the main entrance on Bosbaanweg, there's a bicycle-hire kiosk and visitors centre, **De Boswinkel**, which has maps that are helpful for getting your bearings, and sells tickets for summer boat cruises. By the **Grote Vijver** lake, you'll find canoe, kayak, SUP and pedal-boat rental as well as electric boats for kids to captain.

Over 50km of walking and cycling trails thread through the forest, which also has two horse-riding schools. The **Klimpark Fun Forest** has a ropes course and ziplining through the trees.

Families with littlies in tow will love **De Ridammerhoeve**, an organic working goat farm where children can feed baby goats with bottles of milk in season. Its shop sells goat's-milk ice cream and other products; there are also cheese-making workshops.

During summer, the open-air **Bostheater** stages everything from concerts to Shakespeare and other plays (actors pause for planes to and from nearby Schiphol International Airport as they fly overhead)

Restaurants and cafes are dotted throughout the forest; there's even a campground with cabins and sites to pitch up overnight.

Getting to Amsterdamse Bos

Amsterdamse Bos is an easy bike ride 4.5km southwest of Vondelpark. Buses 347 and 357 run here from Station Zuid and Museumplein.

A fun way to travel here is on a vintage European tram collected between the 1950s and '70s – the earliest date to the 1890s – and run by the **Electrische Museumtramlijn Amsterdam** (Tram Museum Amsterdam; museumtramlijn.org). On Sundays from April to October, Line 30 departs from red-brick Haarlemmermeer Station near Vondelpark to Amstelveen via Amsterdamse Bos. A return trip takes about 1¼ hours; you can hop off at scheduled stops en route.

Discover De Hallen

These red-brick, 1902-built tram sheds were formerly used as a squat before being turned into this breathtaking skylit space. **De Hallen** (Map p108, C1; dehallen-amsterdam.nl) was stunningly converted in 2014 to create a cultural complex incorporating a **food hall** (foodhallen.nl), a brasserie, a library, design shops such as the **Denim City Store** (denimcity.org) and the **Maker Store** (themakerstore.nl), a **bike seller-repairer** (recyclefietsen.nl), a **cinema** (filmhallen.nl) and a hotel.

Regular events held inside include themed weekend markets (such as organic produce or Dutch design).

A lively daily (except Sunday) street market, **Ten Katemarkt** (tenkatemarkt.nl), takes place outside.

Vondelbunker · LIVE PERFORMANCE

23 ⭐ MAP P108, D2

An alternative surprise lying beneath the 1e Constantjin Huygensstraat Bridge: the Vondelbunker. This hidden-away space behind a graffitied door is a fallout shelter dating from 1947, which became Amsterdam's first youth centre in 1968 and was a hotbed of hippie creativity and activism. Today it's a volunteer-run spot for live music, film nights, poetry and more. (vondelbunker.nl)

Lab 111 · CINEMA

24 ⭐ MAP P108, C1

Opened in a former university science laboratory, this cinema screens cult films (in English and Dutch with English subtitles) such as *Enter the Dragon, Taxi Driver, Volver* and *Goodfellas*. Its in-house bar, Strangelove, serves great cocktails and wood-fired sourdough pizzas. (lab111.nl)

Orgelpark · CONCERT VENUE

25 ⭐ MAP P108, C2

A unique performance space for organ music, with four big organs in a lovely restored 1918 Romanesque-style brick church on the edge of the Vondelpark. Around 80 events take place each year, including concerts of classical, jazz and improvised music. (orgelpark.nl)

Shopping

Nixx · CHEESE

26 🔒 MAP P108, D4

Sleek and stylish like the leafy surrounding neighbourhood, Nixx stocks a superb range of Dutch cheeses (eg Nagelkaas, cow's-milk cheese from Friesland made with cloves, and Texelaar, a soft,

Emmenthal-style cheese from the island of Texel) and international varieties. It also roasts nuts in store daily, and sells dried fruit and a small but stellar selection of natural wines. (nixxnotenenkaas.nl)

Donsje — CHILDREN'S CLOTHING

27 🔒 MAP P108, D3

Behind a charming dollhouse-like facade on upmarket Willemsparkweg, this is the original, flagship store of Amsterdam-founded high-end baby- and children's-wear label Donsje. Environmentally sustainable materials and techniques are used to create adorable handmade booties, jumpsuits, trousers, jackets and backpacks with nature themes. Part of its proceeds are donated to children's charity Shining Star Foundation, providing educational opportunities. (donsje.com)

J&B Craft Drinks — DRINKS

28 🔒 MAP P108, C2

J&B Craft Drinks offers a huge range of craft beers, ciders and tasty soda from all over the globe, which are available cold from the fridge, making them perfect to take to the nearby Vondelpark on a hot day. Regular beer and cider tastings take place. (jbcraftdrinks.com)

Salle Privée — PERFUME

29 🔒 MAP P108, D3

Layered fragrances have subtle or lasting sillage (lingering scent), with notes such as wisteria, orange blossom, birch, cedar or opoponax (gum resin that smells like crushed ivy and honey). You can also customise your own distinct fragrance. It was launched by Patrick Munsters, founder of Amsterdam-established global success story, fashion-chain Scotch & Soda. (salle-privee.com)

Patisserie Linnick — CHOCOLATE

30 🔒 MAP P108, B4

Pastry and chocolate get a colourful spin at this modern patisserie shop. The owners Linda van der Lee and Nick van Doorn met and fell in love while serving Dutch snacks at Amsterdam institution Patisserie Holtkamp (p83) and opened their own venture with homemade croissants, macaroons, bars of fair-trade chocolate and romance-inspired bonbons shaped like hearts and kisses. (linnick.nl)

De Winkel van Nijntje — TOYS

31 🔒 MAP P108, F4

A Miffy (Nijntje in Dutch) emporium, devoted entirely to the much-adored character of Dutch illustrator Dick Bruna. The mouthless one is celebrated in all sorts of endearing merchandise, from crocheted dolls to Royal Delft plates. (dewinkelvannijntje.nl)

Explore ✦

De Pijp

A hotbed of creativity, multicultural De Pijp is less than five minutes from Centraal Station by metro yet preserves its village-like atmosphere. The neighbourhood's centrepiece is Amsterdam's largest street market, the colourful Albert Cuypmarkt, and the fashion boutiques, vintage shops, wine bars and free-spirited cafés (pubs) that surround it.

The Short List

○ **Albert Cuypmarkt (p123)** *Feasting your senses at Amsterdam's – and the Netherlands' – biggest street market.*

○ **Sarphatipark (p123)** *Strolling through an urban oasis of lawns, statues and ponds.*

○ **Boaty (p123)** *Casting off in an electric boat to cruise Amsterdam's canals.*

○ **Heineken Experience (p123)** *Taking an interactive, boisterously fun tour of this famous former brewery premises.*

○ **Kaasbar (p124)** *Savouring Dutch cheeses from an elegant sushi-style conveyor belt.*

Getting There & Around

Ⓜ The Noord/Zuidlijn (north–south metro line; M52) serves De Pijp station.

🚋 Tram 24 rolls to/from Centraal Station along Ferdinand Bolstraat. Tram 4 travels from Centraal via Rembrandtplein to De Pijp. Tram 3 traverses De Pijp between Vondelpark and Oost. Tram 12 cuts through De Pijp to/from Leidseplein.

Neighbourhood Map on p122

Albert Cuypmarkt (p123) KIEV.VICTOR/SHUTTERSTOCK ©

Walking Tour 🥾

Discovering Arty De Pijp

With streets named for painters, De Pijp has long been popular with artists and creative entrepreneurs, who have hung out here since the 19th century, when the former slum's cheap housing drew them in. Bohemian flair still wafts through the district, from the cool-cat cafes and retro shops that jam its streets, as well as colourful public artworks.

Walk Facts

Start Jones Brothers Coffee
End Frans Halsstraat
Length 2.2km; three hours

❶ Organic Coffee

Start with a caffeine hit of Amsterdam-roasted organic UTZ (certified sustainable) coffee at **Jones Brothers** (jonesbrothers coffee.com), either at its clutch of tables or to take with you – its cups and lids are 100% plant based. You can also buy beans and composta-ble coffee-machine capsules.

❷ Gnome Sculptures

As you pass the 1884 neo-Gothic mansion **Huis met de Kabouters** at Ceintuurbaan 251, look up to the elaborately carved wooden gables to see two cheeky lime-green goblin sculptures dressed in red hats and shorts; one is holding a red ball and the other is reaching to catch it.

❸ Delftware Street Art on Hemonylaan

The short, narrow tree-lined street **Hemonylaan** has several works of blue-and-white Delftware-style street art by stencil artist Hugo Kaagman. His creations cover sev-eral walls, as well as an electricity building.

❹ De Pijp's Pipes

Henk Duijn's 1993 sculpture **Drie Zuilen** consists of three twisted ceramic 'pipes' (recalling the neigh-bourhood's name, De Pijp, meaning the Pipe, for its narrow streets resembling clay pipe stems). The circa 4.5m-high sculptures are inlaid with glass and brass that reflect the sun and street light at night.

❺ Retro Records

The wonderfully retro **Record Mania** (recordmania.nl) is where locals go for their vinyl and CDs. The shop, with old posters, stained-glass windows, and records and CDs embedded in the floor, is a treasure itself.

❻ Marie Heinekenplein

The Heineken brewery once stood at **Marie Heinekenplein**, yet this public square is named after the founder's cousin, painter Marie Heineken.

❼ Art Supplies

If you're inspired by De Pijp's public art and creative vibes, the neighbourhood's branch of vener-able Dutch art-supply shop **Van Beek** (vanbeekart.nl) is a great place to pick up canvases, brushes, oils, watercolours, pastels, charcoals and more.

❽ Famous Selfies

Wake Me Up When I'm Famous, by Jurriaan and Rinus van Hall, is a 2013 street-art mural with the words stencilled in white on a black background and selfie-favourite bench in front.

De Pijp

A
B
C
D

1

2

3

4

5

6

Vijzelgr
Noorderstr
Nieuwe Looiersstr
Utrechtsedwarsstr
Falckstr
Frederiksplein
Sarphatistr

Weteringschans
1, 7, 19
Lijnbaansgracht
Weteringschans
1, 7, 19, 24
Westeinde
Oosteinde

Stadhouderskade
Weteringcircuit
Hobbemakade
Ruysdaelkade
Boerenwetering

Heineken
Experience
2

Singelgracht
Stadhouderskade
Hemonylaan
Govert
Flinckstr
Hemonystr

1e Jacob van
Campenstr
Bakers &
Roasters
2e Jacob van Campenstr
1e Sweelinckstr
2e Jan Steenstr
2e Jan van der
Heijdenstr

20
19
Ferdinand
Bolstr
6
33
Gerard Doustr
Little
Collins
Van Wou str
Sarphatipark

Daniël Stalpertstr
17
11
*Albert
Cuypmarkt*

32
29
30
10
14
1
28
27
3
Sarphatipark
15
St Willibrordusstr
Ceintuurbaan

De Pijp
Volendammer
Vishandel
Sarphatipark

21
Govert Flinckstr
1e Jan Steenstr
Sarphatipark
*Scandinavian
Embassy*
13
Van Ostadestr

1e Jan van der Heijdenstr
12
9
25
Rustenburgerstr

8
Ceintuurbaan
3, 12, 24
De
Pijp
*Coffee &
Coconuts*
31
22
2e Van der Helststr
1e Van der Helststr

Van Ostadestr
23
Karel du Jardinstr
Tolstr
26

Rustenburgerstr
24
Van der
Helstplein
DE PIJP
Lutmastr
Burgemeester Tellegenstr

Cornelis Troostr
16
Ferdinand Bolstr
De Dageraad
4
Pieter Lodewijk Takstr

Van Hilligaertstr
Hotel Okura
Amsterdam

Jozef Israëlskade
18
Jozef Israëlskade
Amstelkanaal

Amstelkanaal
5
Boaty
Scheldestr

Churchilllaan
12
Churchilllaan

For reviews see	
⊙ Sights	p123
⊗ Eating	p124
⊗ Drinking	p127
☆ Entertainment	p129
⌂ Shopping	p130

N
0 ———— 200 m
0 ———— 0.1 miles

A
B
C
D

Sights

Albert Cuypmarkt

MARKET

1 MAP P122, B3

From Monday to Saturday, some 260 stalls fill the 1905-established Albert Cuypmarkt, Amsterdam's largest and busiest market. Vendors loudly tout their array of gadgets, homewares, flowers, fruit, vegetables, herbs and spices. Many sell clothes and other goods – often cheaper than anywhere else. Snack vendors tempt passers-by with raw-herring sandwiches, *frites* (fries), *poffertjes* (tiny Dutch pancakes) and caramel-syrup-filled *stroopwafels*. If you have room after all that, the surrounding area teems with cosy *cafés* (pubs) and restaurants. (albertcuyp-markt.amsterdam)

Heineken Experience

BREWERY

2 MAP P122, B2

On the company's former brewery site, the Heineken Experience provides an entertaining overview of the brewing process. The 90-minute self-guided visit incorporates a multimedia exhibit where you 'become' a beer by getting shaken up, sprayed with water and subjected to heat; tours include two tastings, and the opportunity to personalise your own Heineken bottle. Upgraded ticket options include the Rooftop experience, viewing the former malt attic and panoramic views over Amsterdam, or Rock the City featuring a 45-minute canal cruise. (heinekenexperience.com)

Sarphatipark

PARK

3 MAP P122, C3

While Vondelpark is bigger in size and reputation, this tranquil English-style park delivers an equally potent shot of pastoral summertime relaxation, with far fewer crowds. Named after Samuel Sarphati (1813–66), a Jewish doctor, businessman and urban innovator, the grounds incorporate ponds, gently rolling meadows and wooded fringes. In the centre is the 1886-built **Sarphati Memorial**, a bombastic temple with a fountain, gargoyles and a bust of the great man himself.

De Dageraad

ARCHITECTURE

4 MAP P122, D5

Following the key *Housing Act* of 1901, which forced the city to rethink neighbourhood planning and condemn slums, De Dageraad housing estate was developed between 1918 and 1923. One of the most original architects of the expressionist Amsterdam School, Piet Kramer, drew up plans for this idiosyncratic complex in collaboration with Michel de Klerk. Plans of De Pijp, floorplans, stained glass, sculptures and photos are displayed at its **Museum De Dageraad**; tickets include a tour of the complex. (dedageraad.nl)

Boaty

BOATING

5 MAP P122, B5

Boaty's location on the peaceful Amstelkanaal makes it an ideal launching pad for exploring the waterways before approaching the crowded city-centre canals. Rental includes a map outlining suggested routes; you don't need a boat licence or prior experience. Its ecofriendly electric boats carry up to six people. It opens year-round, closing 30 minutes before sunset. (amsterdamrentaboat.com)

Eating

Kaasbar

CHEESE €€

 6 MAP P122, B2

Kaasbar is a cheese lover's dream, an elegant restaurant with a sushi-style conveyor belt of artisan cheese winding by diners. Beneath the glass cloches: a range of over 20 Dutch cheeses including white, red, blue and hard, accompanied

Little Collins

BHARAT RAWAL/SHUTTERSTOCK ©

by garnishes. They can all be paired with charcuterie and bread, plus beers or wines by the glass. (kaas bar.amsterdam)

Graham's Kitchen

GASTRONOMY €€€

 7 MAP P122, D2

A veteran of Michelin-starred kitchens, chef Graham Mee now crafts intricate dishes at his own premises. Multicourse menus (no à la carte) might include savoury waffles with black-pearl caviar or slow-cooked veal with riso nero and celeriac. Most produce is organic and sourced from the Amsterdam area; vegetarian menu is available. (grahamskitchen.amsterdam)

Sir Hummus

MIDDLE EASTERN €

 8 MAP P122, A4

Sir Hummus is the brainchild of three entrepreneurial Israelis, who opened a London street-market stall and then their Amsterdam cafe. Creamy, all-natural, preservative- and additive-free hummus is served with pillowy pita bread and salad; SH also makes fantastic falafels and *sabich* (aubergine- and egg-stuffed pitas). You can eat in or take away, but arrive early before it sells out. (sirhummus.nl)

Massimo

GELATO €

9 MAP P122, B4

Gelato is made daily on site from family recipes using local, organic milk, butter and yoghurt along with imported Italian ingredients

Brunch in De Pijp

De Pijp is at the epicentre of Amsterdam's brunch scene. These are our top picks (all take walk-ins).

Bakers & Roasters (Map p122, A2; bakersandroasters.com) Sumptuous brunch dishes include banana-nut-bread French toast; Navajo eggs with pulled pork, avocado, mango salsa and chipotle cream; and a smoked-salmon stack with poached eggs, potato cakes and hollandaise. Wash them down with a fiery Bloody Mary.

Scandinavian Embassy (Map p122, B3; scandinavianembassy.nl) Seasonal dishes – such as oatmeal porridge and blueberries or salt-cured salmon on Danish rye – and freshly baked cinnamon buns make this blond-wood-panelled spot a perfect place to start the day – as does its coffee sourced from Scandinavian micro-roasteries.

Little Collins (Map p122, C2; littlecollins.nl) On a side street near Albert Cuypmarkt, this spot is hopping during brunch, when dishes might include oat-milk panna cotta with rhubarb or poached eggs with smoked labneh and dukka, plus a Bloody Mary with fermented chilli.

Coffee & Coconuts (Map p122, B4; coffeeandcoconuts.com) A 1920s art-deco cinema has been stunningly transformed into this open-plan, triple-level, cathedral-like space. Brunch dishes – including coconut, almond and buckwheat pancakes or French-toast brioche with salted coconut caramel and fresh fruit – are served all day.

such as lemons from the passionate fourth-generation gelato maker's native Liguria. Scrumptious flavours – which may include cinnamon and fig; honey, yoghurt and cherry; and pear and walnut – are scooped with a spatula into hand-rolled waffle cones or tubs. (massimogelato.com)

Butcher

BURGERS €

10 ❌ MAP P122, B3

Burgers at this sizzling spot are flame-grilled right in front of you (behind a glass screen, so you won't get splattered). Mouthwatering choices include Silence of the Lamb (with spices and tahini), the Codfather (beer-battered blue cod and homemade tartar sauce), an Angus-beef truffle burger and a veggie version. (the-butcher.com)

Le Salonard

DELI €

11 ❌ MAP P122, B2

This enticing deli offers high tea with pastries (both savoury – such as quiches, gourmet sandwiches and sausage rolls – and sweet), cheeses, charcuterie, breads and a floor-to-ceiling wall of wines. There are also *borrel* ('drinks') platters of fried snacks to nibble on over vintages by the bottle or glass on the pavement terrace out the front. The vegan sandwiches are lovely. (lesalonard.com)

Sugo
PIZZA €

12 MAP P122, B4

Spectacular pizza slices at this two-storey restaurant are cooked daily, displayed beneath glass and warmed in ovens. Its 20 topping combinations include caramelised onion, mascarpone, walnut and black olive, or potato, mushroom and truffles. Veggies are locally sourced; meats and cheeses are from small farms in Italy. Takeaway packaging is made from recycled paper and energy is 100% sustainable. (sugo.nl)

Surya
INDIAN €€

13 MAP P122, B3

Indian restaurants can be surprisingly hit and miss in this multicultural city, making classy Surya an invaluable address for fans of Subcontinental cuisine. Menu standouts include a feisty madras, a fire-breathing vindaloo, tandoori tikka dishes and silky tomato-based *paneer makhni* with soft cottage cheese made fresh each day. Mains come with pappadams, rice and salad. Its bar serves house-made gin. (surya restaurant.nl)

Spang Makandra
SURINAMESE €

14 MAP P122, A3

There are just 26 seats at this cosy 1978-established restaurant and it's a red-hot favourite with students and the local Surinamese and Indonesian communities – so you'll need to book for dinner. The reward is a fabulous array of dishes including fish soups and satay with spicy sauces at astonishingly cheap prices. All the food is halal; no alcohol is served. (spangmakandra.nl)

Sea Salt & Chocolate
CAFE €

15 MAP P122, D3

This backstreet cafe serves exceptional treats baked fresh on the premises each day. Temptations range from braided babka to cheesecakes in flavours like *speculaas* (spiced biscuit), pecan tarts and signature sea-salt chocolate cake with caramel icing. It also makes cookies (eg red velvet, or vegan choc chip). To re-create them at home, book a three-hour baking workshop (English available). (seasaltandchocolate.nl)

Holland or the Netherlands?

'Holland' is a popular synonym for the Netherlands, yet it only refers to the combined provinces of Noord (North) and Zuid (South) Holland. (Amsterdam is Noord-Holland's largest city; Haarlem is the provincial capital.) The rest of the country is not Holland, even if locals themselves often make the mistake.

Eating Herring Like a Local

'Hollandse Nieuwe' isn't a fashion trend – it's the fresh catch of super-tasty herring, raked in every June. Vendors sell the salty fish all over town. Although Dutch tradition calls for dangling the herring above your mouth, in Amsterdam the fish is served chopped in bite-size chunks and eaten with a toothpick, topped with *uitjes* (diced onions) and *zuur* (sweet pickles). A *broodje haring* (herring roll) is even handier, as the fluffy white roll holds on the toppings and keeps your fingers clean.

Locals flock for a herring fix at **Volendammer Vishandel** (Map p122, B3; volendammervishandeljcmkoning.business.site), which has its own fishing fleet.

Drinking

Brouwerij Troost
BREWERY

16 MAP P122, B5

Watch beer being brewed in stainless-steel vats behind a glass wall at this outstanding organic craft brewery. Beers include a summer blonde and a *tripel* (strong Belgian-style ale) as well as IPAs. It also distils cucumber and juniper gin from its beer and serves a fantastic bar menu (eg pulled-pork nachos) with meat-free options available. Book on weekend evenings. (brouwerijtroost.nl)

Bar Mokum
COCKTAIL BAR

17 MAP P122, B2

An ode to Amsterdam, named for the city's much-loved nickname, Mokum (derived from the Yiddish meaning 'safe haven'), with decor re-creating its timeless streetscapes, this inspired bar mixes cocktails made with local spirits and liqueurs, such as Bols vodka, Damrack *jenever* and De Kuyper Heering cherry liqueur, and has a soundtrack of funk, soul, hip-hop and jazz. (barmokum.nl)

Twenty Third Bar
COCKTAIL BAR

18 MAP P122, B5

High up in the skyscraping Hotel Okura Amsterdam (p130), Twenty Third Bar has sweeping views to the west and south. The adjacent twin-Michelin-starred kitchen of **Ciel Bleu** (cielbleu.nl) also creates stunning bar snacks such as *okonomiyaki* (Japanese savoury pancakes) and foie gras with mango and spiced cake, as well as syrups, purees and infusions for its cocktails. Champagne cocktails are a speciality. (okura.nl)

De Tulp
BAR

19 MAP P122, B2

Festooned with greenery, blooms and fairy lights indoors and out on its huge terrace – a veritable jungle of ivy, ferns, olive trees and palms – de Tulp feels like a giant garden party no matter the weather. Street-food sharing platters (squid-ink calamari, gyoza dumplings, spicy chicken wings...) accompany beers, wines and brimming cocktails. There are regular vinyl and salsa nights. (tulp.amsterdam)

Jacob's Juice   JUICE BAR

20  MAP P122, A2

Reducing food waste was the inspiration behind Jacob's Juice. Its owners collect imperfect fruit and vegetables each day from the Albert Cuypmarkt that stallholders would otherwise discard (an average of 500kg per month). They then transform them into super-healthy juices (like beetroot, carrot and ginger), smoothies (coconut milk, banana and raw cacao) and pickled veggies in recycled jam jars. (jacobs-juice.com)

Café Binnen Buiten   BROWN CAFE

21  MAP P122, A3

The minute there's a sliver of sunshine, this place gets packed. Sure, the food's good and the bar's candlelit and cosy, but what really draws the crowds is simply the best canal-side terrace in De Pijp – an idyllic spot to while away an afternoon. (cafebinnenbuiten.nl)

GlouGlou   WINE BAR

22  MAP P122, C4

Natural, all-organic, additive-free wines are the stock-in-trade of this

Rialto Cinema

convivial neighbourhood wine bar in a rustic stained-glass-framed shop, where the party often spills out onto the street. More than 40 well-priced French wines are available by the glass; it also sells bottles to drink on site or take away. No reservations. (glouglou.nl)

Café Ruis BAR

23 MAP P122, C4

Opening to one of the liveliest terraces on plane-tree-shaded square Van der Helstplein, Ruis has a stylish yet cosy interior with board games plus a kids' toybox and colouring books. Craft beers are on tap; homemade food includes *bitterballen* (deep-fried croquettes) to accompany *borrel*. (cafe-ruis.nl)

Gambrinus BROWN CAFE

24 MAP P122, B4

Named for legendary medieval European figure King Gambrinus, renowned for his love of beer and brewing, this congenial split-level *café*, with giant windows and a street-side terrace, is a local favourite. Look out for its own brews. (gambrinus.nl)

Entertainment

Rialto Cinema CINEMA

25 MAP P122, B4

Opened in 1920, this art-deco cinema near Sarphatipark shows eclectic arthouse fare from around the world (foreign films have Dutch

Startup Scene

Many successful Amsterdam businesses – from beer, such as **Brouwerij Troost** (p127), to burgers, like the **Butcher** (p125), among numerous other enterprises – put down their first roots in De Pijp. This innovative neighbourhood has a constant turnover of pop-ups, startups and new openings. Along with the main drags, backstreets to watch include Frans Halsstraat, 1e Van der Helststraat, 2e Van der Helststraat, Cornelis Troostplein and Ruysdaelkade, as well as tucked-away square Van der Helstplein.

or English subtitles). Tickets can be purchased online or at the box office. There are three screens and a stylish on-site cafe. (rialtofilm.nl)

Cinetol ARTS CENTRE

26 MAP P122, D4

With a capacity of just 150, cultural centre Cinetol is an intimate place to catch established and emerging local acts across all musical genres: garage, post-punk, Afrobeat, jazz and electronic dance music. It also hosts art exhibitions, film screenings, market days and album launches. Its on-site cafe has a sunny terrace. (cinetol.nl)

The Netherlands' Largest Barometer

Rising 75m above low-rise Amsterdam, the landmark **Hotel Okura Amsterdam** (Map p122, B5; okura.nl) building is visible from afar both day and evening. Each night the roof's perimeter is illuminated by LED lights, which change colour depending on the barometer's reading for the following day. Blue lights mean a bright, sunny day is forecast. Green lights mean bad weather is on the way. 'White' (more like a pale, pinkish colour, and the most common) means the weather will be changeable.

The lights also change colour on special occasions, producing a variegated rainbow effect for **Queer & Pride Amsterdam** (p29) and New Year's Eve, and, of course, turning orange for the Netherlands' national holiday **King's Day** (Koningsdag; 27 Apr), a celebration of the House of Orange, with hundreds of thousands of orange-clad locals and visitors filling Amsterdam's streets for drinking, dancing and buying and selling secondhand wares when the city becomes one big flea market.

Shopping

Bier Baum
DRINKS

 27 🔒 MAP P122, B3

Perfect for Sarphatipark picnic supplies, Bier Baum has fridges keeping many of its craft beers and ciders chilled. Look out for Dutch brews such as Amsterdam's Brouwerij Poesiat & Kater and Brouwerij 't IJ, Haarlem's Uitje Brewing Co and Nijmegen's Oersoep, and international beers from as far afield as New Zealand and Hawaii. (bier-baum.nl)

Cottoncake
CONCEPT STORE

28 🔒 MAP P122, B3

Painted cotton-white inside and out, this chic little shop stocks fashion, jewellery and homewares from Dutch designers Yaya and Mimi et Toi as well as international labels. It also makes its own scented candles and perfumes, and has a small cafe on its mezzanine where you can stop for homemade cakes, waffles, freshly squeezed juices and Amsterdam White Label coffee. (cottoncake.nl)

Mercer
FASHION & ACCESSORIES

29 🔒 MAP P122, A3

The Amsterdam-based label Mercer focuses on sustainable streetwear such as satin varsity jackets and vegan sneakers made from pineapple leather, Italian grapes or plastic waste collected from the ocean. All pieces are designed locally and made in sustainably certified factories. (merceramsterdam.com)

De Pijp Shopping

't Kaasboertje

FOOD & DRINKS

30 🔒 MAP P122, B3

Enormous wheels of Gouda line the walls of this enticing cheese shop, and more cheeses fill the glass display cabinet. Crispbreads and crackers are on hand, as well as wines (reds, whites and rosés) from the Netherlands, Belgium and Germany. (facebook.com/tKaasboertjeAmsterdam)

Grice

FASHION & ACCESSORIES

31 🔒 MAP P122, C4

This small, light-filled boutique is the showroom of Amsterdam Fashion Academy graduate Joanna Grice, whose ethos is using her sewing machine as a paintbrush, and focus is sustainability. Grice employs zero-waste patternmaking techniques and recycled and upcycled fabrics to create unique pieces such as dresses, tunics and jackets that can be worn in different ways. (joannagrice.com)

Blond

GIFTS & SOUVENIRS

32 🔒 MAP P122, A3

In a Barbie-pink shop that doubles as a tearoom, the owners sell plates and dishes that they glaze in colourful, often hilarious designs – ladies lunching, beach scenes, cakes and chocolates – that make great gifts for anyone who likes modern kitsch with a sense of humour. Sweet treats such as lemon meringue tarts are served on Blond's own crockery. (blond-amsterdam.com)

Blond

Penny Lane

VINTAGE

33 🔒 MAP P122, B2

Style icons from the swinging '60s and '70s such as Brigitte Bardot, Audrey Hepburn, Paul Newman and David Bowie are the inspiration for the hand-picked, high-end clothing, bags, accessories and footwear at this vintage boutique. Along with bold, bright mid-century patterns, there are also more classic pieces from designers like Valentino, Etro, Montgomery, or Guy Laroche. (pennylanevintage.nl)

Explore

Oosterpark & East of the Amstel

Oost (East) is one of Amsterdam's most culturally diverse neighbourhoods. It grew up in the 19th century, with grand buildings and wide boulevards, and is now rapidly gentrifying, with hip bars, boutiques and restaurants popping up. The large English-style Oosterpark was laid out in 1861, while the lush expanses further east date from when this area was a country retreat.

The Short List

○ **Wereldmuseum Amsterdam (p134)** *Browsing the World Museum's thought-provoking exhibitions.*

○ **Dappermarkt (p138)** *Sniffing out Turkish pide (topped flatbread), kebabs and olives at Dapper-markt's food stalls.*

○ **Oosterpark (p138)** *Watching wild parakeets and herons in this peaceful park.*

○ **De Kas (p138)** *Dining in the greenhouse that grew the ingredients for your meal.*

○ **Canvas (p142)** *Clinking glasses to the sweeping city views from this rooftop bar.*

Getting There & Around

🚃 From Centraal Station, tram 14 skirts Oosterpark's northern edge en route to Flevopark. Trams 1, 3 and 19 run past Oosterpark on their east–west routes across the city.

Ⓜ Lines 51, 53 and 54 run south from Centraal Station; the Wibautstraat stop is close to the Oost's southwest edge.

Neighbourhood Map on p136

Oosterpark (p138) DEBELLI92/SHUTTERSTOCK ©

Top Experience 📷

Discover world cultures at the Wereldmuseum Amsterdam

With roots in a 19th-century collection covering Dutch overseas territories, and, later, the Artis Zoo's ethnographical collection and tropical research, the galleries of the Wereldmuseum Amsterdam surround a huge central hall across three floors and present multimedia exhibits with insight and imagination.

◎ **MAP P136, C2**

World Museum
Amsterdam

amsterdam.
wereldmuseum.nl

Galleries

The museum's permanent collection, **Things That Matter**, explores the importance of objects and items such as clothing and nostalgic music to heritage, looking at issues such as climate change and migration.

There are also excellent **temporary exhibits**, which can range from subjects like cultural appropriation (through symbols, clothing, hairstyles, dance, music and language) or the changing relationship with plastic around the globe.

Wereldmuseum Junior

The museum has a kids' section, **Wereldmuseum Junior**, aimed at youngsters from six to 13 years of age. It's great for hands-on fun, with loads of interactive exhibits.

Building History

This monumental arched building, rising over three levels around its light-flooded, glass-roofed great hall, was commissioned in 1910. When it opened in 1926, the building was Amsterdam's largest. Incredibly, during the WWII occupation of Amsterdam, both the Nazi police and the Resistance operated from here.

Prior to late 2023, it was known as the Tropenmuseum, before changing its name to become the Wereldmuseum Amsterdam. It's now in partnership with the Wereldmuseum Berg en Dal (previously the Afrika Museum), the Wereldmuseum Leiden (previously the Museum Volkenkunde) and the Wereldmuseum Rotterdam.

Global Gifts

The museum's gift shop stocks enticing and unusual arts and crafts; it also has an online store.

★ Top Tips

o Unlike many major Amsterdam museums, pre-booking isn't essential (you can buy tickets when you arrive). But, especially at peak times, it's still a good idea to buy tickets ahead of time online to avoid any queues.

o The museum is wheelchair accessible, with an elevator.

✕ Take a Break

Opening to a lovely terrace overlooking the Oosterpark, the museum's **cafe** fittingly serves global cuisine, with a kids' menu available, too.

Alternatively, duck across the road to **Louie Louie** (louie louie.nl) for laid-back brasserie food in a convivial setting, with a glass-covered terrace for all weather.

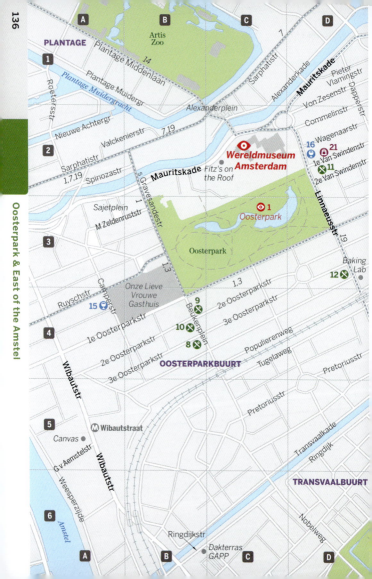

A   B   C   D

PLANTAGE

Artis Zoo

Plantage Middenlaan

7

1

Plantage Muidergr

Plantage Muidergracht

Roeterstr

Nieuwe Achtergr

Valckenierstr

7,19

Sarphatistr

Sarphatistr

1,7,19

Spinozastr

Alexanderplein

Mauritskade

Pieter Vlamingstr

Von Zesenstr

Commelinstr

Wagenaarstr

16   21

1e Van Swindenstr

11

2e Van Swindenstr

2

Wereldmuseum Amsterdam

Fitz's on the Roof

S Gravesandestr

Sajetplein

M Zeldenruststr

1

1

Oosterpark

Oosterpark

Linnaeusstr

19

Baking Lab

12

3

Onze Lieve Vrouwe Gasthuis

1,3

Campensstr

Ruyschstr

15

1e Oosterparkstr

2e Oosterparkstr

3e Oosterparkstr

9

Beukenplein

10

8

2e Oosterparkstr

3e Oosterparkstr

OOSTERPARKBUURT

Populierenweg

Tugelaweg

Pretoriusstr

4

Wibautstr

5

Wibautstraat

Canvas

G v Aemstelstr

Wibautstr

Pretoriusstr

Transvaalkade

Ringdijk

TRANSVAALBUURT

Nobelweg

6

Amstel

Weesperzijde

Ringdijkstr

Dakterras GAPP

A   B   C   D

E Zeeburgerdijk

Zeeburgerdijk F Zeeburgerdijk G H

× 7

17

Molukkenstr

1

Pontanusstr

Timorplein

Bankastr

Madurastr

Javastr

Balistr

DAPPERBUURT

INDISCHE
BUURT

Borneostr

14

Sumatrastr

Celebesstr

Javastr

× 6

Javaplein

1e Atjehstr

2 Dappermarkt

1e Atjehstr

Insulindeweg

2

Dapperplein

2e Atjehstr

Riaowstr

13

Reinwardtstr

3

Molukkenstr

Insulindeweg

Wijttenbachstr

Muiderpoort

Celebesstr

3

Molukkenstr

Celebesstr

Polderweg

18

Atlantisplein

14

Celebesstr

4

Waldenlaan

20

Linnaeuskade

Archimedesweg

Molukkenstr

Linnaeusstr

Hogeweg

Linnaeusparkweg

Middenweg

19

N 0 200 m
0 0.1 miles

5

× 5

Park
Frankendael

3

19

4

Frankendael
House

Middenweg

E F G H

For reviews see

◎ Top Experiences	p134
◉ Sights	p138
⊗ Eating	p138
◉ Drinking	p141
☆ Entertainment	p142
🔒 Shopping	p143

6

Sights

Oosterpark
PARK

1 MAP P136, C3

The Oosterpark's lush greenery, with wild parakeets in the trees and herons stalking the large ponds, brings an almost tropical richness to this diverse neighbourhood, despite being laid out in English style. Designed by Leonard Antonij Springer, it was established in 1891 as a pleasure park, and still retains an elegant, rambling feel. Tango sessions take place on alternate summer Sundays in the wrought-iron bandstand. Families will enjoy the playground (with a summer wading pool) on the park's north side.

Dappermarkt
MARKET

2 MAP P136, E2

The busy, untouristy Dapper-markt is a swirl of life and colour, with around 250 stalls. It reflects the Oost's diverse immigrant population, and is full of a medley of shoppers and vendors selling foods (apricots, olives, fish, Turkish kebabs) and goods, from costume jewellery to cheap clothes at stalls lining the street. (dappermarkt.nl)

Frankendael House
HISTORIC BUILDING

3 MAP P136, F6

This area was rolling countryside several centuries ago. In the 18th century, wealthy Amsterdammers would pass their summers and weekends in large country retreats on a tract of drained land called Watergraafsmeer. There were once around 40 such mansions, but the last survivor is Franken-dael, an elegant, restored Louis XIV–style mansion. There's a free open house on the last Sunday afternoon of the month when you can explore the building. Art exhibitions often take place here. (huizefrankendael.nl)

Park Frankendael
PARK

4 MAP P136, E6

Sprawling over 7 hectares, these lovely, landscaped gardens are the grounds of a former country estate; the mansion, Frankendael House, is still standing and there are walking paths, nesting storks, decorative bridges and the remains of follies. The excellent De Pure Markt (p143) is held here on the last Sunday of each month. (huizefrankendael.nl)

Eating

De Kas
INTERNATIONAL €€€

5 MAP P136, E6

In a row of stately 1926 greenhous-es, De Kas has an organic attitude to match its chic glass setting. It grows most of its own produce right here and the result is incred-ibly pure flavours and innovative combinations. The daily menus (three or four courses at lunch, five or six at dinner) are based on what-ever has been freshly harvested. (restaurantdekas.com)

Wilde Zwijnen

DUTCH €€

6  MAP P136, H2

The name means 'wild boar' and there's usually game served at this modern Dutch restaurant. With cream-coloured walls and reservations scrawled in chalk on wood tables, the restaurant has a pared-down, rustic-industrial feel, and serves locally sourced, seasonal dishes with a creative twist. Its daily three- to five-course menus (no à la carte) are either meat, fish or vegetarian. (wildezwijnenwinkel.nl)

Pompstation

DUTCH €€€

7 MAP P136, F1

Opening to a vine-draped terrace, this 1912 pumphouse building is a wonderful example of the Amsterdam School architectural style. Its cavernous interior is a splendid setting for three- to five-course menus featuring Dutch produce like wild Waddenzee scallops and oysters, dry-aged Holstein beef, Texel lamb, and for-aged mushrooms and herbs. Live jazz plays on Friday and Saturday evenings. (pompstation.nu)

Merkelbach

CAFE €€

The Merkelbach cafe sits in the coach house adjoining Frankendael House (see **3** Map p136, F6), and has a terrace perfect for summer alfresco dining overlooking Frankendael's formal gardens. Its small but stellar all-vegetarian lunch menu spans soups such as artichoke and garlic, salads including bread-based panzanella with string beans and burrata, and pastas like spinach

Dappermarkt

Baking Bread

Breathe in the aroma of fresh baking in this open **Baking Lab** (Map p136, D3; bakinglab. nl) with a red-brick wood-fire oven recalling the spirit of the old communal bakery, where people brought dough to knead and put in the shared oven, as few houses had their own. It offers breadmaking workshops (English available); there are also workshops for children.

You can also pop in to snack on vegetarian pastries, quiches, sandwiches and cakes.

and ricotta ravioli with Sorrento lemon. (restaurantmerkelbach.nl)

Clos   TAPAS €€

 MAP P136, B4

Creative, constantly changing tapas-style dishes using ingredients from small farms and artisan producers, such as asparagus with wild-garlic *bitterballen* (deep-fried croquettes), smoked mackerel with turnip foam or octopus with chorizo, complement Clos' 100-plus natural wines from small-scale, family-run vineyards. (closamsterdam.nl)

Het IJsboefje   ICE CREAM €

 MAP P136, B4

There's a joy-filled atmosphere around Het IJsboefje, a popular ice-cream stop close to Oosterpark that's been going strong since 1957. There are benches outside; inside it serves satisfyingly big portions of delicious flavours such as *stroopwafel* (caramel wafer), fig and walnut, blueberry cheesecake, orange and coriander or limoncello. You can also get milkshakes, and hot or iced coffee. (facebook.com/hetijsboefje)

Erik's Delicatessen   DELI €

10 MAP P136, B4

Put together a gourmet Oosterpark picnic with Dutch and European cheeses, charcuterie, fresh bread, tapenades, olives, salads and canned and bottled preserves, vinegars and oils, as well as a fantastic range of wines. (eriksdelicatessen.nl)

Roopram Roti   SOUTH AMERICAN €

11 MAP P136, D2

This simple canteen-style Surinamese cafe often has a queue out the door, but it moves fairly fast. Place your order at the counter – the scrumptiously punchy and flaky lamb roti 'extra' (with egg) and the *barra* (lentil doughnut) are winners – and don't forget the fiery hot sauce. It's super-delicious for takeaway or to eat at its handful of communal tables. (roopramroti.nl)

Freddy Fryday   FAST FOOD €

12 MAP P136, D3

Head to Oosterpark with a recycled box or cone of homemade fries piled high with gourmet toppings: pulled pork, parmesan truffle or cheesy mushroom; there are 14 additional sauces. Around half its variations, like the 'Freddy's Nachos', are vegetarian. It also whips up rich milkshakes in flavours such as vanilla, strawberry, coconut or banana. (freddyfryday.nl)

Drinking

Distilleerderij 't Nieuwe Diep
DISTILLERY

13 MAP P136, H2

Appearing out of the woods like a *Hansel and Gretel* cottage, the quaint architecture and setting of this old pumping station, with a lakeside terrace next to an orchard, make it feel like a magical countryside retreat. The distillery makes around 100 small-batch *jenevers* (Dutch gins), herbal bitters, liqueurs and fruit distillates from organic ingredients according to age-old Dutch recipes. (nwediep.nl)

Brouwerij Poesiat & Kater
MICROBREWERY

14 MAP P136, F4

Salted-caramel miso stout and hibiscus ruby ale are some of the inventive creations brewed on site at this microbrewery. Inside the soaring brick warehouse it has a spiral staircase leading to a mezzanine and 12m mural of the brewing process from fermentation to mashing and toasting. Outside is a huge waterside terrace perfect for sampling its wares. (poesiaten kater.nl)

4850
WINE BAR

15 MAP P136, A4

From your morning caffeine and cinnamon- or cardamom-bun fix to an evening tipple with New Nordic sharing plates, hip cafe-wine-bar 4850 has you covered. It turns out great Scandinavian-sourced coffee along with an impressive

Football Fever

High-tech complex **Johan Cruijff ArenA** (johancruijffarena.nl), 7km southeast of central Amsterdam and reached by metro, is the home of four-time European champions Ajax, the Netherlands' most famous football team. The 1996-opened stadium was renamed from the Amsterdam ArenA in 2018 after the legendary footballer Johan Cruijff (1947–2016), the country's greatest player.

When no games are on, fans can tour the 68,000-capacity stadium with a retractable roof (there's a tour for children too) and visit the World of Ajax museum, with memorabilia including jerseys, trophies, ticket stubs and player contracts, and commemorative Delftware porcelain. The arena also hosts big-name live-music shows, as do neighbouring venues AFAS Live and Ziggo Dome.

selection of wines displayed across the rear wall. Natural light floods the industrial-meets-mid-century interior; the outdoor pavement area is the ideal spot for sunny days. (4850.nl)

De Biertuin
BEER GARDEN

16 MAP P136, D2

With a covered terrace and heaters for chillier weather, 'the beer garden' is perennially popular with locals for its lengthy beer list (18 on tap, including three house collaborations, and over 100 more Dutch and Belgian varieties in bottles) and great pub food, such as burgers, glazed ribs and rotisserie chicken. (debiertuin.nl)

Entertainment

Studio K
ARTS CENTRE

17 ⭐ MAP P136, G1

This hip Oost arts centre always has something going on, with a cinema, a nightclub, a stage for bands and a theatre. There's also an eclectic restaurant, serving sandwiches and salads for lunch and vegetarian-friendly, international dishes for dinner, and a huge terrace. (studio-k.nu)

Oost's Rooftop Bars

Oost has a trio of rooftop bars perfect for a sundowner.

Canvas (Map p136, A5; volkshotel.nl) Zoom up to the Volkshotel's trendy 7th-floor bar for some of the best views in town, either through its large windows or on the open terrace. DJs spin on Friday and Saturday nights year-round. On summer evenings, it often has open-air cinema screenings and the opportunity for a dip in one of the rooftop hot tubs.

Dakterras GAPP (Map p136, B6; hotelcasa.nl) On the Hotel Casa's 8th floor, Dakterras GAPP is framed by a glass railing for uninterrupted views over Oost's rooftops and canals. Its wooden-decked terrace, with picnic tables and furniture made from upcycled timber pallets, is bordered by a herb garden that provides the ingredients for cocktails and bar food to accompany 40 different Dutch beers.

Fitz's on the Roof (Map p136, C2; fitzsbaramsterdam.com) From the Pillows Maurits hotel's umbrella-shaded 4th-floor terrace, Fitz's on the Roof, you can look out over Oosterpark, the Wereldmuseum Amsterdam and Artis Zoo. European championship-winning cocktails are inspired by the 1920s, for example Essence No 5 (a twist on fragrance Chanel No 5, with sandalwood- and vanilla-infused gin, rose liqueur and peach soda, and perfume atomiser with orange-blossom liqueur).

Q-Factory
LIVE MUSIC

18 MAP P136, E4

Rock, metal, soul, funk, electronica and dance events all raise the roof at this 700-capacity venue. It's part of a complex that also houses recording studios, music offices and a cafe and hotel. (q-factory-amsterdam.nl)

Shopping

De Pure Markt
MARKET

19 🔒 MAP P136, E6

On the last Sunday of the month De Pure Markt sets up in Park Frankendael (p138), with artisanal and organic producers selling delicious gourmet foodstuffs. Browse the wares with a coffee or craft beer in hand, then grab a bite from the food stalls. Quality arts and crafts include handwoven rugs, wooden chopping boards and fashion made from recycled materials. (puremarkt.nl)

Het Faire Oosten
GIFTS & SOUVENIRS

20 🔒 MAP P136, E4

The perfect place to pick up an interesting gift or souvenir, Het Faire Oosten is stocked with beautiful homewares, quirky books, accessories and clothing by designers with an emphasis on sustainability.

Musical Roots

Oosterpark plays host to a number of lively events during the summer and it's a great place to get a feel for the multicultural makeup of the neighbourhood. One highlight is the free global-music performances held on an open-air stage as part of the weeklong **Roots Festival** (amsterdamroots.nl), which usually takes place in late June to early July at various venues around town.

You might find cool raincoats made from recycled plastic bottles, fair-trade wooden kitchen utensils, vegan leather-look bags and eco-conscious, fashionable clothing made from organic cotton. (hetfaireoosten.nl)

We Are Vintage
VINTAGE

21 🔒 MAP P136, D2

This packed-to-the-gills shop has a great range of good-quality secondhand threads. It has a regular turnover; you might come across anything from '70s Thea Porter boho chiffon dresses or colourful Bill Gibb knitwear to '80s Guess denim jeans and jackets and '90s shirts and sportswear. (rumoursvintage.nl)

Explore

Nieuwmarkt, Plantage & the Eastern Islands

Buzzing Nieuwmarkt is rich with history. Here you'll find Rembrandthuis – the master painter's studio – and insightful museums in centuries-old synagogues in the old Jewish quarter. Leafy Plantage is home to the zoo and botanical gardens, while the Eastern Islands have maritime history, warehouses turned hip bars and flagship modern Dutch architecture.

The Short List

○ **Museum Rembrandthuis (p146)** *Viewing Rembrandt's former home and studio.*

○ **Het Scheepvaartmuseum (p152)** *Fathoming Dutch seafaring history through this maritime collection.*

○ **Muziekgebouw aan 't IJ (p159)** *Catching live jazz or classical at this acoustically and visually stunning venue.*

○ **Verzetsmuseum (p152)** *Discovering personal stories of the Dutch Resistance to WWII occupation.*

Getting There & Around

🚊 Tram 14 goes to Waterlooplein and the Jewish Cultural Quarter, and Plantage. Tram 7 goes to the Eastern Islands and Eastern Docklands. Tram 26 traverses the IJ River waterfront.

Ⓜ Lines 51, 53 and 54 stop at Waterlooplein and Nieuwmarkt.

Neighbourhood Map on p150

Waag (p149) WUT_MOPPIE/SHUTTERSTOCK ©

Top Experience 📷

Explore Museum Rembrandthuis

Museum Rembrandthuis provides unique insight into one of the greatest Dutch artistic geniuses, Rembrandt van Rijn. Occupying the canal house where he lived at the height of his success, the museum's interiors have been reconstructed from a detailed inventory made when Rembrandt left the house after his fortunes took a dive.

◎ MAP P150, B4

Rembrandt House Museum

rembrandthuis.nl

The House

The house dates from 1606. Rembrandt bought it for a fortune in 1639, made possible by his wealthy wife, Saskia van Uylenburgh. Multimedia-guided visits start on the lower level in the kitchen, with tobacco pipes and other objects unearthed during the renovation. Rembrandt's ground-floor former showroom has repurchased paintings and sculptures once owned by the artist.

Studio & Cabinet

Climb the narrow staircase and you'll come to the master's light-filled studio. Facing north and offering ideal light, this is where he painted masterpieces such as *The Night Watch* (1642). Artists give demonstrations here on how Rembrandt sourced and mixed paints.

Across the hall is Rembrandt's 'Cabinet', a room crammed with curiosities like those he collected: seashells, glassware, Roman busts and stuffed alligators.

Etchings

A small room is devoted to Rembrandt's famous etchings. The museum has a near-complete collection of them (about 250), although they're not all on display at once. Demonstrators crank up an oak press to show etching techniques several times daily.

Bankruptcy

The house was ultimately Rembrandt's financial undoing. As his work fell out of fashion, he was unable to pay off the mortgage, and in 1656 the house and its effects were sold to compensate his creditors. It's thanks to the debt collector's itemised list that the museum has been able to reproduce the interior so authentically. Rembrandt lived the rest of his years in cheaper digs in the Jordaan.

★ Top Tips

○ Tickets must be reserved in advance, when you'll need to choose a timeslot.

○ Early or late in the day are the quietest times to visit, especially midweek.

○ The modern wing, including the entrance, exhibition galleries and workshop space and museum shop are wheelchair accessible, but Rembrandt's home is only accessible by steep staircases.

○ The free multimedia guide offers interesting details and insights.

○ Check the schedule for etching workshops.

✕ Take a Break

Have lunch at light-filled cafe **TisFris** (tisfris.nl), only a few doors away.

Linger over a canal-side drink and snack at 17th-century **De Sluyswacht** (p158), a charmingly wonky building right on the waterfront.

Walking Tour

Exploring Nieuwmarkt & Plantage

Nieuwmarkt's action-packed plaza and Plantage's garden-district greenery make for lively and lovely strolling. Distinctive cafes are the bonus here: they pop up in rustic shipping warehouses, 17th-century lock-keepers' quarters, the turreted city gate and just about everywhere in between. A flea market adds to the daily buzz.

Walk Facts

Start De Druif
End Scheepvaarthuis
Length 3.5km; two hours

❶ Stop in at De Druif

In a building dating from 1566, **De Druif** (cafededruif.nl), meaning 'the Grape' gained its first liquor licence in 1631, and acted as an embarkation *café* (pub), where sailors came to register for work on Dutch East India Company (VOC) ships. Its time as a former distillery is evident in its wooden spirit barrels behind the bar.

❷ Dockside at Entrepotdok

The Dutch East India Company, which grew rich on sea trade in the 17th century, owned **Entrepotdok**, a 500m row of warehouses that was the largest storage depot in Europe at the time. It's now packed with offices, apartments and dockside cafes perfect for lazing away a few hours at the water's edge, looking across to the Artis Zoo.

❸ Wertheimpark's Memorial

Opposite the Hortus Botanicus, **Wertheimpark** is a willow-shaded spot brilliant for relaxing by the Nieuwe Herengracht – it's a great place to escape the crowds for a while. On the park's northeast side, locals often place flowers at the Auschwitz Memorial, a panel of broken mirrors installed in the ground that reflects the sky.

❹ Flea Market Finds

Covering the square once known as Vlooienburg (Flea Town) daily except Sunday, the **Waterlooplein Flea Market** (waterlooplein. amsterdam) draws sharp-eyed customers seeking everything from antique knick-knacks to designer knock-offs and cheap bicycle locks in among some tourist tat. The street market started in 1880, when Jewish traders living in the neighbourhood started selling their wares here.

❺ Amsterdam's Historic Waag

The **Waag** was built as a gate in the city walls in 1488. In 1601 the walls were demolished as the city expanded and the building was turned into Amsterdam's main weigh house – then a spot for public executions. A bar-restaurant occupies it today. The masons' guild was based in the tower facing the Zeedijk; note the superfine brickwork. Out front, Nieuwmarkt hosts a variety of events, including a Saturday farmers market.

❻ Scheepvaarthuis

Finish your walk with a nose around the supreme example of the Amsterdam School, **Scheepvaarthuis** (Shipping House; amrathamsterdam. com), with its nautical motifs, masterly stained glass and beautiful art-deco cafe. It's now open to guests as the Grand Hotel Amrath, but staff are happy for tourists to look around.

A B C D

1

Prins Hendrikkade

Centraal Station

De Ruijterkade

Oosterdoksstr

24

OBA: Centrale Bibliotheek Amsterdam

22

Oosterdokskade

9 **30**

15

Damrak

Zeedijk

Gelderskade

Prins Hendrikkade

Oosterdok

2

Beursstr

Warmoesstr

MEDIEVAL CENTRE

Stormst

Binnen Bantammerstr

Binnen

Binnenkant

Waalseilandsgracht

Oude Waal

Oudezijds Voorburgwal

Oudezijds Achterburgwal

Tokoman

Bloedstr

29

3

Nieuwmarkt

NIEUWMARKT

Koningsstr

Oude Schans

25

Peperstr

12

Rapenburg

Koestr

34

Keizersstr

23

Nieuwmarkt

33

St Antoniesbreestr

Oude Schans

Oude Hoogstr

Nieuwe Hoogstr

Nieuwe Uilenburgerstr

Uilenburgergracht

Oost-Indisch Huis

10

4

Zandstr

Kloveniersburgwal

Museum Rembrandthuis

21

Jodenbreestr

Valkenburgerstr

Anne Frankstr

Verversstr

Zwanenburgwal

32

Waterlooplein

Portuguese Synagogue

Rapenburgerstr

Nieuwe Herengracht

Plantage Parklaan

Staalstr

Mr Visser-plein

Muiderstr

Plantage

14

Stopera

27

Tokoman

Nieuwe Amstelstr

Joods Museum

Wertheim-park

Fortius Botanicus

1

19

Binnen Amstel

Amstel

Waterlooplein

National Holocaust Museum

5

Hortusplantsoen

Hollandsche Schouwburg

For reviews see
- Top Experiences p146
- Sights p152
- Eating p154
- Drinking p157
- Entertainment p159
- Shopping p161

Nieuwe Herengr

Nieuwe Keizersgr

Weesperstr

Nieuwe Keizersgr

Nieuwe Kerkstr

Plantage

Amstel

6

16

A B C D

E
26
28

F

G

H

1

Piet Heinkade

26

Jollemanhof

IJHaven

Veemkade

Javabrug

17

Dijksgracht

Dijksgracht

Piet Heinkade

31

IJ Tunnel

2

3 **NEMO Science Museum**

Kattenburg

Kattenburgerstr

OOSTELIJKE EILANDEN (EASTERN ISLANDS)

Wittenburg

3

Historic Barges

Het Scheepvaartmuseum

8 **Arcam**

2

Kattenburgerplein

Grote Wittenburgerstr

Kleine Wittenburgerstr

Schippersgr

Kadijkspl

Nieuwevaart

Wittenburgergr

11

Oostenburgervoorstr

4

Laagte Kadijk

Overhaalsgang

Plantagekade

Entrepotdok

Hoogte Kadijk

Nieuwe Vaart

Oostenburgergr

Oostenburgerstr

Czaar Peterstr

Verzetsmuseum

4

Entrepotdok

Funenkade

5

Zeeburgerstr

20

7

PLANTAGE

5 **Artis Zoo**

6 **Micropia**

13

7 **Groote Museum**

18   14

Artis Zoo

Sarphatistr

Alexanderkade

Mauritskade

6

Plantage Kerklaan

Plantage Middenlaan

Plantage Muidergr

Muidergracht

Von Zesenstr

E

F

G

H

Sights

Hortus Botanicus
GARDENS

 1 MAP P150, D5

A botanical garden since 1638, the 1.2-hectare Hortus Botanicus bloomed as tropical seeds and plants were brought in by Dutch trading ships. From here, coffee, pineapple, cinnamon and palm-oil plants were distributed throughout the world. Its medicinal gardens provided the Netherlands' doctors with remedies. The gardens' 4000-plus species occupy wonderful structures including a 1911 palm house, butterfly house and three-climate glasshouse being renewed as the world's first fully sustainable, climate-neutral greenhouse in 2024. The 1875 orangery shelters a lovely cafe. (dehortus.nl)

Het Scheepvaartmuseum
MUSEUM

 2 MAP P150, E3

A waterfront 17th-century admiralty building houses this state-of-the-art presentation of maritime memorabilia. Highlights include imaginatively presented Golden Age maps, fascinating 19th-century photos of early voyages and an immersive audiovisual journey evoking a sea voyage. There's plenty to keep kids interested, too. Outside, you can clamber over the full-scale replica of the 700-tonne *Amsterdam* – one of the largest ships in the Dutch East India Company fleet – with its tiny bunks and sailors' hammocks, and admire the Royal Barge in the boathouse. (Maritime Museum; hetscheepvaartmuseum.nl)

NEMO Science Museum
SCIENCE CENTRE

 3 MAP P150, E2

Perched atop the entrance to the IJ Tunnel is this unmissable green-copper building with a slanted roof, designed by Italian architect Renzo Piano and almost surrounded by water. Its rooftop square has great views and water- and wind-operated hands-on exhibits. Inside, everything is interactive, with four floors of investigative mayhem that kids of all ages will enjoy. Experiment with lifting yourself up via a pulley, making bubbles, building structures, racing your shadow, watching a chain-reaction display and discovering the teenage mind. (nemosciencemuseum.nl)

Verzetsmuseum
MUSEUM

4 MAP P150, E5

The museum of the Dutch Resistance brings the horror of German occupation in WWII vividly alive, using personal stories, letters, artefacts, films and photographs to illuminate local resistance to the Nazis. Its modernised permanent exhibition, *The Netherlands in WWII*, chronicles armed resistance, people who helped those in hiding, forged documents, underground news services and general strikes. The excellent Verzetsmuseum Junior puts the war into context for kids through the eyes of four Dutch children. Compelling temporary exhibitions regularly take place. (verzetsmuseum.org)

Artis Zoo ZOO

5 MAP P150, E5

Founded in 1838, Artis is one of Europe's oldest zoos. Its 14 leafy hectares are home to over 750 animal species, from lions, jaguars, elephants and giraffes to sealions, golden-cheeked gibbons, iguanas, flamingos and cassowaries. There's a reptile house, several aviaries, and an aquarium (undergoing renovations at the time of writing). The butterfly pavilion has more than a thousand flittering creatures. You can journey through the solar system and Milky Way at the 324-seat planetarium (included in zoo admission). (artis.nl)

Micropia MUSEUM

6 MAP P150, E5

The world's first microbe museum is a germaphobe's nightmare. Micropia has hands-on exhibits, microscopes to peer through and fascinating, if unsettling, facts about how many living organisms there are around us every day. Dare to take a body scan and become acquainted with your own microorganisms. Learn the unromantic side of locking lips via the kiss-o-meter. There are also glass models of viruses from Ebola to smallpox. Combination tickets are available with neighbouring Artis Zoo. (micropia.nl)

Hortus Botanicus

MARIEKE THISSEN/SHUTTERSTOCK ©

Groote Museum MUSEUM

 7 MAP P150, E5

Adjacent to Artis Zoo (p153), with combination tickets available, the Groote Museum opened in 2022. It highlights the connection between humans and other lifeforms. Each of its 14 interconnected zones focuses on a different part of the human body; you'll discover, for instance, how your vocal chords produce sound and the difference between your voice and that of a chimpanzee. (grootemuseum.nl)

Arcam ARCHITECTURE

 8 MAP P150, E3

The curved Amsterdam Architecture Foundation is a striking waterside building designed by Dutch architect René van Zuuk. It hosts changing architectural exhibitions, often focused on urban design in Amsterdam. Check the online agenda for informative guided architectural tours of the city on foot or by bike. (Stichting Architectuurcentrum Amsterdam; arcam.nl)

OBA: Centrale Bibliotheek Amsterdam LIBRARY

9 MAP P150, D2

This being Amsterdam, it has one of the coolest libraries you can imagine, built in 2007 and spread over multiple light, bright floors. The basement is devoted to kids, with low shelves of books, activities, a polar bar and a display case with dolls of diverse nationalities, skin colours and physical abilities. On the 7th floor is a 250-seat cinema, a cafe and restaurant with an outdoor summer terrace offering thrilling panoramic views across the water to Amsterdam's medieval centre. (oba.nl)

Oost-Indisch Huis ARCHITECTURE

10 MAP P150, A4

The mighty Dutch East India Company (Vereenigde Oostindische Compagnie; VOC), founded in 1602, was one of the earliest multinational companies, trading spices, opium and more with Asia. This imposing red-and-white edifice is the company's former office, built between 1551 and 1643 and attributed in part to Hendrick de Keyser, the busy city architect. The VOC sailed into rough waters and was dissolved in 1798. The building is now owned by the University of Amsterdam.

Eating

Frank's Smoke House SEAFOOD €€

11 MAP P150, G4

Frank is a prime supplier to Amsterdam's restaurants, and you can try his renowned smoked fish and meats at this smart deli-restaurant. Delicious takeaway sandwiches (smoked halibut, truffle cheese or warm smoked ham with relish) are available from the deli, or dine in on smoked-fish platters, king crab or smoked brisket, along with excellent beer featuring smoked malt. (smokehouse.nl)

Jewish Amsterdam

Jewish Origins

Nieuwmarkt's Jewish quarter evolved after Spain and Portugal's expulsion in the 1580s brought a large number of Sephardic (Jews of Spanish, Middle Eastern or North African heritage) refugees. Barred from numerous professions by monopolistic guilds, some Jewish people were diamond cutters (which had no guild), and others introduced trades like printing or worked in unrestricted industries such as finance. Unlike elsewhere in Europe at the time, Jews were permitted to buy property as civic authorities didn't want to restrict such productivity.

In the 17th century, Ashkenazim (Jews from Europe outside of Iberia) arrived, fleeing pogroms in Central and Eastern Europe. By Napoleonic times, Amsterdam was Europe's largest Jewish centre.

During French rule, the guilds and remaining restrictions on Jews were abolished, and Amsterdam's Jewish community thrived in the 19th and early 20th centuries.

WWII Devastation

The Nazis' devastation of Amsterdam's Jewish community was near-total. Before the war, some 90,000 Jews lived in Amsterdam (13% of the city's population). Shockingly, only 5500, scarcely one in 16 people, survived the war.

Estimating the current population is complex, however it's thought the Netherlands has a core Jewish population of some 30,000 people, around half of whom live in Amsterdam.

The city's motto, *Heldhaftig, Vastberaden, Barmhartig* (Valiant, Steadfast, Compassionate), presented by Queen Wilhelmina in 1947, commemorates its citizens' protests against the persecution of Jewish people in WWII.

Jewish Cultural Quarter

Amsterdam's **Joods Cultureel Kwartier** (Jewish Cultural Quarter; jck.nl) brings together four major sites accessible on one ticket – the **Joods Museum** (Map p150, C5), **Portuguese Synagogue** (Map p150, C5), **Hollandsche Schouwburg** (Holland Theatre; Map p150, D5) memorial and, at the former Hervormde Kweekschool, where hundreds of Jewish children were saved during the war, the **National Holocaust Museum** (Map p150, D5).

Gebr Hartering

DUTCH €€€

12 ✕ MAP P150, C3

Lined in rustic wood, with elegant white-clothed tables and views overlooking gabled canal houses, this gem was founded by two food-loving brothers, who offer five- to seven-course menus that change daily according to the best seasonal produce available. A meal here is always a delight to linger over, so settle in and enjoy the accompanying wines and peaceful waterside location. (gebr-hartering.nl)

De Plantage

EUROPEAN €€

13 ✕ MAP P150, E5

Huge and graceful, this is an impressive space in an 1870s-built, 1900-expanded former greenhouse decked with blond wood

De Plantage

and black chairs and views of Artis Zoo's aviary. Food is fresh and creative, including fennel-sausage-filled ravioli or mackerel ceviche with garden peas, radish and pickled daikon. In summer, the loveliest tables are on the terrace beneath trees strung with fairy lights. (caferestaurantdeplantage.nl)

Sterk Staaltje

DELI €

14 ✕ MAP P150, A5

With pristine fruit and veg stacked up greengrocer-style outside, Sterk Staaltje is worth entering just for the aroma of its foodstuffs, with a tantalising range of ready-to-eat treats: Spanish chicken with butterbeans and artichoke, spinach and pumpkin quiche, filling salads and hearty soups. The sandwiches are fantastic – chargrilled steak with Parmesan cheese and homemade pesto or smoked salmon and avocado on focaccia. (sterkstaaltje.com)

Sea Palace

CHINESE €€

15 ✕ MAP P150, C2

In stark contrast to its surrounds, this floating pagoda-style Chinese restaurant has three floors busy with locals and visitors here for the great views of the city from across the IJ, and for the extensive and delicious menu, from Peking-duck pancakes to outstanding dim sum (served until 4pm). It seats a whopping 600 people, but reservations are still recommended. (seapalace.nl)

Mama Makan
INDONESIAN €€

16 MAP P150, D6

What looks like a nondescript brick building from the outside opens to a spectacular, jungle-style space with bamboo, hanging plants, jade-green banquettes and a vertical garden beside the bar. Mama Makan's menu ranges from Indonesian market snacks (eg tempeh fritters) to bountiful *rijsttafels* ('rice tables'; Indonesian banquets) of vibrant dishes to share. (mamamakan.com)

Mediamatic ETEN
VEGAN €€

17 MAP P150, E1

Art, design and life sciences hub Mediamatic has a sustainability focus and striking waterside bar/restaurant using produce from its on-site greenhouses. It serves bar snacks and four-course vegan dinner menus that might feature ginger olive bread with black-pepper crumble or masala potato muffins with beetroot fries and horseradish cream. (mediamatic.net)

Box Sociaal
INTERNATIONAL €€

18 MAP P150, E5

Set up by two Aussies, this stylish neighbourhood cafe opposite Artis Zoo has you covered any time of the day. Brunch dishes like smashed avo on toast, Benny & the Jets (eggs Benedict) and Throw Another Shrimp on the Bagel (prawn toast) are served all day. Dinner takes things up a notch, for instance hake with mango and charred-corn salsa. (boxsociaal.com)

Surinamese Sandwiches

Queue with the folks getting their Surinamese spice on at **Tokoman** (Map p150, B5; tokoman.nl). It makes a sensational *broodje pom*, a sandwich filled with a tasty mash of chicken and a starchy Surinamese tuber. You'll want the *zuur* (pickled-cabbage relish) and *peper* (chilli) on it, plus a cold can of coconut water to wash it down.

There's another **branch** (Map p150, B3) close by.

Café Smit en Voogt
CAFE €€

19 MAP P150, D5

On a leafy corner, with high ceilings and a relaxed vibe, this cool and laid-back cafe is ideal for a salad like goat's cheese and grilled veggies or sandwich such as pastrami, pickles and mustard mayo for lunch, or simply a coffee and slice of apple pie when visiting nearby sights like the Museum het Rembrandt Huis or Hortus Botanicus. (cafesmitenvoogt.nl)

Drinking

Brouwerij 't IJ
BREWERY

20 MAP P150, H5

Can you get more Dutch than drinking a beer beneath the creaking sails of the 1725-built De Gooyer windmill? Amsterdam's leading microbrewery makes delicious standard, seasonal and limited-edition brews, with 11 on tap. Enjoy them in the tiled tasting room, lined by an amazing bottle collection, or plane-tree-shaded terrace. English tours run at 3.30pm Friday to Sunday. (brouwerijhetij.nl)

De Sluyswacht BROWN CAFE

21 MAP P150, B4

Out on a limb by the canal and listing like a ship in high winds, this tiny black building dating to 1695 was once a lock-keeper's house on the Oude Schans. The canal-side terrace with views of the Montelbaanstoren is a charming spot to relax with a frothy Dutch beer and bar snacks, including *bitterballen* (deep-fried meatballs), chips and toasties. (sluyswacht.nl)

Hannekes Boom BEER GARDEN

22 MAP P150, D2

Reachable via a couple of pedestrian/bike bridges from the NEMO Science Museum, this laid-back waterside cafe is built from recycled materials and has a huge beer garden. Join the crowd enjoying the sunshine at brightly coloured picnic tables or cosy into an armchair by the fire inside. The site dates to 1662, when guards here monitored maritime traffic. (hannekesboom.nl)

Rosalia's Menagerie COCKTAIL BAR

23 MAP P150, A3

Rosalia's is spectacularly styled like a Golden Age seafaring tavern with its rich floral wallpaper, plush armchairs, framed old maps, and trinkets and curiosities like sailors once brought back from voyages. Expertly made tipples focus on Dutch heritage, including *jenever*-based cocktails, accompanied by a small bar menu (brisket *bitterballen*, dried Dutch sausage, pepper pâté). Reserve a table ahead on weekends. (rosalias. amsterdam)

LuminAir COCKTAIL BAR

24 MAP P150, C1

A 360-degree panorama of Amsterdam unfolds from the 11th floor of the DoubleTree Amsterdam Centraal Station hotel – and gets even better from the vast terrace with an outdoor bar. Luminous projections, cloud-like installations and cocktails such as Halogen Spotlight (samphire-infused tequila and watermelon) or Clear Blue Sky (bergamot, violet liqueur and champagne) are inspired by the different gradients of light. (luminairamsterdam.com)

HPS COCKTAIL BAR

25 MAP P150, D3

Art-deco lights, climbing rose-patterned wallpaper, chesterfields and waistcoated bar staff set the scene at the sophisticated yet cosy HPS (Hiding in Plain Sight). The alchemist mixologists produce concoctions such as Bears & Bees (cucumber-infused vodka with honey and rhubarb liqueur) or I Have Spoken (calvados, Strega

Amsterdam's Golden Age

The Golden Age covers roughly the 17th century, when Amsterdam was at the peak of its powers. It's the era when Rembrandt painted, when city planners built the canals and when Dutch ships were a force to be reckoned with around the world.

It started when trading rival Antwerp was retaken by the Spaniards in the late 16th century, and merchants, skippers and artisans flocked to Amsterdam. A new moneyed society emerged. Not only did persecuted Jews who fled Portugal and Spain introduce the diamond industry to Amsterdam, they also knew of trade routes to the West and East Indies.

Enter the Dutch East India Company, which wrested the Asian spice trade from the Portuguese. It soon grew into the world's richest corporation, with more than 50,000 employees and a private army. Its sister, the Dutch West India Company, traded with Africa and the Americas and was at the centre of the American slave trade. In 1672 Louis XIV of France invaded the Low Countries, and the era known as the Dutch Golden Age ended.

liqueur and kiwi syrup), and the service is warm and friendly. (hpsamsterdam.com)

Entertainment

Muziekgebouw aan 't IJ
CONCERT VENUE

26 MAP P150, E1

A dramatic glass-and-steel box on the IJ waterfront, this multidisciplinary performing-arts venue hosts over 250 concerts a year, spanning classical to world and electronica. Its state-of-the-art main hall with a flexible stage layout and great acoustics, accommodates 725 people; there's a 100-seat small hall, and intimate jazz stage, Bimhuis. (muziekgebouw.nl)

Nationale Opera & Ballet
CLASSICAL MUSIC

27 MAP P150, B5

The Nationale Opera & Ballet (previously the Muziektheater) is home to the Netherlands Opera and the National Ballet, with some wonderful performances at its 1600-seat auditorium. It presents around 14 opera and 11 ballet productions a year; the season runs from September to June. (operaballet.nl)

Bimhuis
JAZZ

28 MAP P150, E1

The riverside Bimhuis at the Muziekgebouw aan 't IJ is the Netherlands' most important jazz venue. It draws international jazz greats, along with hosting world music and

Worth a Trip:
IJburg

At Amsterdam's eastern edge, IJburg is an archipelago of artificial islands home to one of Amsterdam's newest neighbourhoods and the city's only beach.

The city of Amsterdam first started construction on these islands in the IJmeer lake in 1996 to ease a housing shortage, and the first IJburg residents arrived in 2002. Work is underway on its second phase; ultimately, a total of 18,000 homes for 45,000 residents will be spread across the archipelago.

IJburg's architecture, highlighted by the iconic **Sluishuis** apartment building, showcases modern design, blending contemporary residential structures with sustainable practices and thoughtfully crafted urban spaces.

Beach & Water Sports

Head here on a warm sunny day, when you can take advantage of **Strand Blijburg**, a sweep of imported white sand at IJburg's eastern end (1km east of IJburg's tram stop). It's a fantastic place to go windsurfing or paddleboarding.

Surfcenter IJburg (surfcenterijburg.nl) rents windsurfers from its shipping container. **Amsterdam Watersports** (amsterdamwatersports.com) has flyboarding, wakeboarding, e-foiling, waterskiing, and SUP, sailboat and motorboat rental.

Drinking & Dining

IJburg has a great concentration of restaurants, cafes and bars, especially around its boat-filled marina, just north of the tram stop.

Standouts include bar/restaurant **NAP** (napamsterdam.nl) on Krijn Taconiskade, named for the Normaal Amsterdams Peil, Amsterdam's sea-level benchmark, with a sunny dockside terrace. Overlooking the marina from above is the panoramic **Sky Bar** (fourelementshotel.com/skybar), on the 12th floor of the Four Elements hotel.

Getting to IJburg

IJburg is a 20-minute tram ride on line 26 from Centraal Station (less than 10 minutes from the Eastern Islands) or around 30 minutes by bike.

From April to October, ferries operate from IJburg's marina to Muiden's medieval castle, the Muiderslot, and fortress island, Pampus. Visit amsterdamtouristferry.com for details.

other genres. There are 245 seats plus 139 standing places. Free jam sessions take place on Tuesday nights from September to June (bimhuis.nl)

Amsterdams Marionetten Theater
PUPPETRY

29 ⭐ MAP P150, B3

An enchanting enterprise that seems to exist in another era, this marionette theatre presents fairy tales and Mozart operas, such as *The Magic Flute,* in a former blacksmith's shop. Kids and adults alike are enthralled by the magical stage sets, period costumes and beautiful singing voices that bring the diminutive cast to life. (marionettentheater.nl)

Conservatorium van Amsterdam
CLASSICAL MUSIC

30 ⭐ MAP P150, D2

Catch a classical, jazz or acoustic recital by students at the Netherlands' largest and most prestigious music academy. There are regular festivals in this snazzy contemporary building adjacent to the city's main library, the OBA: Centrale Bibliotheek (p154). (conservatoriumvanamsterdam.nl)

Mezrab – House of Stories
PERFORMING ARTS

31 ⭐ MAP P150, H2

This wonderfully eclectic harbourside cultural centre hosts storytelling sessions (mainly in English), Iranian rock bands, hip-swinging Latin American bands, European folk dances, open-mic comedy nights and much more from all corners of the world. (mezrab.nl)

Shopping

DSign
DESIGN

32 🔒 MAP P150, A5

Vividly coloured Dutch design products at this upmarket boutique include tulip bags by ByLin, Gobi sunglasses, Secrid wallets and purses, Thijs Verhaar scarves, Nijntje (Miffy) lamps and toys, and Rijkje jewellery. (dsign.amsterdam)

RecordFriend Elpees
MUSIC

33 🔒 MAP P150, B4

Light, bright and airy, this record shop sells secondhand vinyl (LPs and singles), CDs and vintage turntables. Jazz, blues, soul, reggae and pop are the main genres but you never know what you'll find as you browse. (recordfriendamsterdam.nl)

Jacob Hooy & Co
COSMETICS

34 🔒 MAP P150, A3

A proper apothecary shop, lined by dark wooden drawers and rounded barrels with their contents inscribed in flowing font, Jacob Hooy & Co has been selling medicinal herbs, homeopathic remedies and natural cosmetics since 1743. It also now sells a range of body lotions, herbal teas and essential oils. (jacobhooy.nl)

Explore ◈

Amsterdam Noord

Amsterdam Noord, a quick free ferry ride across the IJ River from central Amsterdam, is a previously neglected spot that has been reinvented as the city's hippest neighbourhood. It encompasses ex-industrial areas, including once-derelict shipyards, cutting-edge architecture and cavernous hangars turned hipster hangouts with walls covered in street art, all minutes away from fields, horses and the odd windmill.

The Short List

○ **A'DAM Tower (p167)** *Taking in the view from this skyscraper.*

○ **EYE Filmmuseum (p167)** *Admiring the angular, gleaming white architecture of the IJ-side Eye, with its cinema-focused exhibitions.*

○ **NDSM Loods (p167)** *Exploring the artist studios in this massive former warehouse.*

○ **Straat (p167)** *Ogling graffiti wonders at the world's largest museum for street art.*

Getting There & Around

⚓ Free 24-hour passenger/bicycle ferries link the rest of the city with Noord every 10 to 15 minutes. Key routes are NDSM to/from Centraal Station and Pontsteiger (Houthavens); and Buiksloterweg to/from Centraal. Between Buiksloterweg and NDSM, it's often quicker to return and change ferries at Centraal than wait for buses.

Ⓜ The north–south line 52 links Amsterdam Zuid in the south with Noorderpark and Noord stations via Amsterdam Centraal Station.

Neighbourhood Map on p166

Cycling Tour

Street Art & Shoreside Ride

Noord is the city's most up-and-coming area, a creative hotbed packed with contemporary art and industrial hangouts by the water's edge. The district is quite spread out – hiring a bike is the smartest way to explore.

Walk Facts

Start Pllek

End Sexyland World

Length 6km

❶ Coffee & Shipping Containers

At hip Noord magnet **Pllek** (pllek.nl), all ages hang in interiors made from shipping containers and lounge on the artificial beachfront. It's a terrific spot to start the day with coffee or breakfast.

❷ Graffiti Hunting

Around NDSM-plein, graffiti abounds on the warehouses. Heading towards Ms van Riemsdijkweg, you'll see artist Eduardo Kobra's gigantic 240-sq-metre, vibrantly multicoloured Anne Frank mural at the entrance to street-art museum **Straat** (p167).

❸ Art Attack

Enter the sprawling **NDSM Loods** (p167), a former shipbuilding warehouse filled with scores of artists' studios, and climb the winding scaffolding stairs to its gallery, NDSM Fuse. Exhibitions explore topical subjects from climate change to gender.

❹ Rummaging Around

Head to the small alley off Papaverweg to reach **Van Dijk & Ko** (vandijkenko.nl). The antique warehouse is packed to the brim with curios – posed mannequins, garden gnomes, a wall of cuckoo clocks and more.

❺ High-Tech Art

Visit the futuristic **NXT Museum** (p168) where art and technology intersect. Larger-than-life installations explore virtual realms with moving lights and sound – absorbing it all takes an hour or two.

❻ Wine Tasting

Sip a glass of wine (or a tasting flight of seven) at the Netherlands' first urban winery, **Chateau Amsterdam** (chateau.amsterdam). Don't forget to peek around the production facility.

❼ Riverside Relaxing

Relax on the waterside terrace (screened by glass from the wind) of **Sexyland World** (sexyland.world) or see what's on the agenda of this unique arts centre/club venue. It has 365 co-owners, each of whom puts on an annual event. There's a Sichuan restaurant and fantastical touches such as a bubblegum-inspired bar designed by local artists.

Noord on Two Wheels

The best way to explore Noord is by bike. Places are spread out, there isn't much traffic and there are lots of cycle routes. Hire a bike at Noord (there are outlets at NDSM or Buiksloterweg ferry wharves), or around Centraal Station and take it for free on the ferry.

For reviews see

⊙	Sights	p167
⊗	Eating	p168
⊙	Drinking	p170
⊙	Entertainment	p171
⊙	Shopping	p171

NIEUWENDAM

Nieuwendammerdijk

8 WH Vliegenbos

Waddenweg

Johan van Hasseltweg

14
17

Nieuwe Leeuwarderweg

Noordhollandsch kanaal

Gedempt
Hamerkanaal

Aambeeldstr

7 Wondr

Noordwal

16

Het IJ

0   0.5 miles
0   1 km

BUIKSLOOT

Schoenmakersweg

Noorderpark

Meidoornweg

Noorderweg

Noorderpark M

NOORD

Mosplein

Meidoornweg

IJ Tunnel

IJplein

Klaprozenweg

Korte
Papaverweg

13

Van der
Pekstraat

9 11

12

Bijlmersteeg

Badhuiskade

IJ Tunnel

Papaverweg

NXT
Museum

18 6

Asterweg

IJpromenade

Buiksloterweg

19

A'DAM
Tower

4

Filmmuseum

EYE 5

IJplein

IJpleinveer

Centraal
Station

NDSM Loods

20 3
NDSM-plein

NDSM-werf ⊙ 1

2
Straat

10

Neveritaweg

15

Ms van

Riemsdijkweg

Het IJ

Distelweg

NDSM-werf

Distelkade

Van Diemenstr

Westerdoksdijk

Galgenstr

Haarlemmer Houttuinen

Brouwersgr

Houttuinen

Planciusstr

Houttuinen

21

Sights

NDSM-werf
AREA

1 MAP P166, B1

Named for the Nederlandsche Dok en Scheepsbouw Maatschappij (the Netherlands Dock & Ship-building Company, which operated here from 1946–79), this derelict shipyard turned edgy arts community has a post-apocalyptic vibe. Abandoned trams rust by the water's edge, and street art is splashed on most surfaces. Creatives hang out at cool cafes, bars and restaurants, and businesses such as MTV have their European headquarters here. The area is also a centre for underground culture and events. (ndsm.nl)

Straat
MUSEUM

2 MAP P166, B1

Follow the smell of fresh paint to the world's largest museum for graffiti and street art. More than 150 works created on-site are spread across an 8000-sq-metre former warehouse. Guided tours and graffiti workshops are available. Check the website for tickets to the Straatstukken nights when live music and painting bring exhibition spaces alive. (straatmuseum.com)

NDSM Loods
ART STUDIO

3 MAP P166, B1

This former shipbuilding warehouse is filled with over 80 studios, with some 250 artists working in the NDSM *broedplaats* (breeding ground). It's a big enough space that you can cycle or walk around the area, with huge artworks hanging from the ceiling and structures within the hangar. Upstairs is an exhibition space, NDSM Fuse. There's a small performance space; expos and events also regularly take place here. (Art City NDSM; ndsmloods.nl)

A'DAM Tower
TOWER

4 MAP P166, C4

The 22-storey A'DAM Tower (1971) was the Royal Dutch Shell oil-company offices, but it's had a makeover to become one of Amsterdam's biggest attractions. Take the trippy lift to the sky deck for sweeping city views in all directions, with a giant six-person swing that kicks out over the edge for those who have a head for heights (you're well secured and strapped in). An Amsterdam VR Ride takes you on a wild simulated roller-coaster ride through the historic city. (adamlookout.com)

EYE Filmmuseum
MUSEUM

5 MAP P166, B4

A modernist architectural triumph on the banks of the IJ (also pronounced 'eye') River, the EYE film museum peers over the city. Its permanent exhibition, *What is Film?*, lets you see how the earliest cameras worked, insert yourself into a film using greenscreen technology, or make your own animated movie. There are in-depth temporary exhibitions. Vintage classics to current blockbusters and kids' films screen at its four cinemas. The view-tastic EYE bar/restaurant has floor-to-ceiling windows and a fabulously sunny riverside terrace. (eyefilm.nl)

NXT Museum
MUSEUM

6 MAP P166, C3

At this new media-art museum in a 1400-sq-metre warehouse space, technology is used to channel creative expression. Artists, scientists, sound engineers, coders and designers collaborate to create an immersive digital experience of light, sound and movement using cutting-edge tech such as robotics, facial recognition, AI and VR. Immense installations with lights and sound immerse guests in otherworldly visits exploring virtual worlds and digital identity. (nxtmuseum.com)

Wondr
ARTS CENTRE

7 MAP P166, D3

You can't miss this gigantic pastel-pink building on Meeuwenlaan. The interactive art experience playspace is a paradise for kids and adults, especially Instagrammers. There are pits for swimming in Styrofoam 'marshmallows' and coloured balls, a pink bouncy castle, confetti room, art installations packed with teddies and more. Outside is a 'beach' complete with pink sand. Admission can be combined with the 'Roller Dreams' pop-up for a disco party under neon lights. Also here is a cocktail bar and cafe. (wondrexperience.com)

WH Vliegenbos
FOREST

8 MAP P166, E3

Dating back over a century, this 20-hectare forest is Amsterdam's oldest, with elm, ash and black alder trees and birdlife including woodpeckers, kingfishers, falcons and blackbirds. Walking and cycling trails weave through the greenery and past ponds and waterways. It's named for Willem Hubert (WH) Vliegen, a municipal city planner, who insisted that a large green space be created for residents arriving in the area; planting began in 1912.

Eating

Proeflokaal Kef
CHEESE €€

9 MAP P166, C3

Specialising in Dutch and French cheese since 1953, Fromagerie Kef has a few shops around town, and here, you can both buy and sample the goods at its adjacent tasting room. Book ahead for cheese tastings with wine or opt for a sandwich filled with Dutch-aged sheep's cheese and fig compote or a cheese platter, paired with a craft beer. (abrahamkef.nl)

Contrast
GASTRONOMY €€€

10 MAP P166, A1

Aboard a former cargo ship moored at NDSM, famed Basque chef Iñaki Bolumburu crafts wholly sustainable fine-dining menus, for instance featuring squid tartare with green-olive emulsion or charred cabbage with potato and pine shoots. There's an art gallery below deck. (contrast.amsterdam)

Dolzon

BAKERY €

11 MAP P166, C3

Dolzon supplies many restaurants in Amsterdam Noord with its fabulous sourdough loaves (varieties include 10 seed, fig, olive and sundried tomato, and hazelnut and raisin), You can pick them up here at its bakery, along with sweet treats such as lemon-curd muffins and apple pie.

Cafe Modern

GASTRONOMY €€€

12 MAP P166, C3

Don't be fooled by the simplistic mid-century decor in this former bank – Cafe Modern is serious about its gastronomy, without a hint of stuffiness. The five- to seven-course set dinner menus incorporate fresh seasonal ingredients in dishes such as Waddenzee oysters with samphire, or hazelnut-crusted quail. (modern amsterdam.nl)

Moon

DUTCH €€€

Tour Amsterdam from your table with a 360-degree panorama over Amsterdam from this revolving restaurant at the top of the A'DAM Tower (see 4 ◉ Map p166, C4). Modern Dutch menus – either sea- and land-based or vegetarian – change with the seasons, with three to five courses at lunch, and four to six courses at dinner (wine pairings available). There's one revolution an hour. (restaurantmoon.nl)

A'DAM Tower (p167)

Festival Over the IJ

Huge performing-arts events (dance, theatre, music, poetry and crossovers with visual and digital art) take place in venues indoors and outside around the NDSM-werf former shipyards during the **Over het IJ Festival** (overhetij.nl) for 10 days in July.

Drinking

Café de Ceuvel   CAFE

13 🚇 MAP P166, C2

Tucked in a former shipyard and designed by architect Wouter Valkenier, this entirely off-grid waterside spot is built out onto an island and constructed from recycled materials. With drinks including homemade lemongrass and ginger soda, plus bottled beer from local breweries, it's a wonderful oasis alongside the canal. Sustainability is also a feature of its kitchen (all food is vegan). (deceuvel.nl)

Shelter   CLUB

In the basement of A'DAM Tower (see **4** 🎯 Map p166, C4), this raw, industrial space with a capacity of 700 is an awesome place to dance to house and techno beats, with local and international DJs and one of the city's best sound systems and light shows. Club nights normally run to 6am on weekends, with regular three-day nonstop events

thanks to the 24/7 licence. (shelter amsterdam.nl)

Garage Noord   BAR

14 🚇 MAP P166, E3

With its industrial setting (a former mechanic shop), this laid-back venue has a rough-around-the-edges feel. Around 10.30pm the space transforms from a casual cafe, restaurant and bar into a club playing host to a changing line-up of DJs. (garagenoord.com)

Noorderlicht   CAFE

15 🚇 MAP P166, B1

In a soaring greenhouse-like structure built from salvaged materials, with grassy waterside lawns and a mini stage, Noorderlicht has a pub-garden-meets-festival vibe. A big play area outside makes it great for families. Its 100% circular ethos of reuse and recycling extends to its organic coffee, craft beers, natural wines, botanical cocktails and predominantly vegan food. (noorderlichtcafe.nl)

Lowlander   BAR

16 🚇 MAP P166, D4

Walk through an industrial complex on Gedempt Hamerkanaal to find Lowlander in a plant-filled former warehouse on the waterfront, with a sun-soaked, south-facing terrace. It brews its own botanical beers, such as lager and lemongrass or ale with orange and dragon fruit, and serves local, seasonal food such as cauliflower and tahini ravioli. (restaurant.lowlander.nl)

Skatecafe BAR

17 MAP P166, E3

At this expansive, warehouse-like restaurant, an indoor skate ramp means you can enjoy drinks while watching skaters do tricks (or do them yourself). There's a regular programme of live music and DJ sets spanning genres from acid jazz to Afrobeats. (skatecafe.nl)

Entertainment

De Ruimte ARTS CENTRE

18 MAP P166, C2

This arts centre hosts a changing roster of events from jazz and poetry to experimental electronica, as well as live music you can put your dancin' shoes on for – Ethiopian jazz, rock 'n' roll, brass bands. Friday nights are usually club nights with DJs. (cafederuimte.nl)

Tolhuistuin LIVE PERFORMANCE

19 MAP P166, C4

In what was the Shell workers' canteen for 70 years from 1941, the nifty Tolhuistuin arts centre hosts African dance troupes, spoken word, theatre and much more on its garden stage under twinkling lights. Club nights and big-name gigs also take place here. There's a waterfront cafe, 1st-floor restaurant and weekend taco bar in the garden. (tolhuistuin.nl)

Shopping

IJ Hallen MARKET

20 MAP P166, B1

This whopping flea market takes place one weekend a month (Saturdays and Sundays), with hundreds of stalls selling vintage clothes, antiques, vinyl, art and much, much more outside in a huge area at NDSM-werf. It moves indoors into two NDSM warehouses from October to March. Numerous food trucks park up here. Check the website for the schedule. (ijhallen.nl)

Neef Louis Design VINTAGE

21 MAP P166, C1

A huge warehouse full of vintage, designer and industrial furniture, this is a trove of antique luggage, midcentury bookcases, retro radios, neon signs and all sorts of other treasures. (neeflouis.nl)

Survival Guide

Concertgebouw (p114) LEONID ANDRONOV/SHUTTERSTOCK ©

Before You Go

Book Your Stay

○ Book as far in advance as possible, especially for festival, summer and weekend visits.

○ There's often a minimum stay of two or three nights, especially at weekends and during major events.

○ Properties often include the 7% *toeristenbelasting* (tourist tax) in quoted rates, but ask before booking. If you're paying by credit card, some hotels add a surcharge of up to 5%.

Useful Websites

Lonely Planet (lonely planet.com/the-nether lands/amsterdam/hotels) Top recommendations.

I amsterdam (iamster dam.com) Wide range of options including short-stay apartments from the city's official website.

Hotels.nl (hotels.nl) For deals on larger properties.

Amsterdam

°C/°F Temp   Rainfall inches/mm

When to Go

Spring (Mar–May) Tulip time! Crowds amass around King's Day (27 April). Alternating rainy and gorgeous weather.

Summer (Jun–Aug) Peak season, warm with long daylight hours, cafe terraces boom, festivals aplenty.

Autumn (Sep–Nov) Can be rainy, generally less busy, the regular cultural season starts up.

Winter (Dec–Feb) The fewest crowds. Ice-skating fun and cosy candlelit cafes ease the dark, chilly days.

Serviced apartments Portals include Short Stay Group (short staygroup.com) and ServicedApartments.nl (servicedapartments.nl).

Best Budget

Cocomama (cocomama hostel.com) Red-curtained boutique hostel in a former brothel.

Generator Amsterdam (staygenerator.com) Designer hostel overlooking Oosterpark.

Bunk (wearebunk.com) Trendy sleeping pods in a converted church.

ClinkNoord (clink hostels.com) Arty, avant-garde hostel in Amsterdam Noord.

Best Midrange

Sweets Hotel (sweets hotel.amsterdam) Live like Amsterdam's bridge keepers once did in one of 28 converted canal-bridge houses.

Hotel Fita (fita.nl) Sweet little family-owned hotel

a stone's throw from the Museumplein.

Conscious Hotel Westerpark

(conscioushotels.com) Eco innovations include recycled materials at this Westerpark hotel inside a national monument.

Linden Hotel

(lindenhotel.nl) Small designer rooms (with a tiny lift) in a central Jordaan canal-side location.

Best Top End

Ambassade Hotel

(ambassade-hotel.nl) Golden Age canal houses shelter this exquisite hotel displaying original CoBrA art.

Dylan (dylanamsterdam. com) An 18th-century jewel with bespoke furnishings.

Hotel de L'Europe Amsterdam

(deleurope. com) Opulent 19th-century hotel on the Amstel with a pool.

Zoku (livezoku.com) Loft spaces for serviced apartment-style living with full kitchens and innovative design touches.

Arriving in Amsterdam

Schiphol Airport

Train From Schipol (schiphol.nl) trains run to Centraal Station (€5.90 one way, 15 minutes) 24 hours a day. From 6am to 12.30am they go every 10 minutes or so; hourly in the wee hours. The rail platform is inside the terminal, down the escalator.

Bus Connexxion Bus 397/Amsterdam Airport Express from 5.23am to 12.11am (every eight minutes) or Connexxion Bus N97 from 1.16am to 4.46am (both services €6.50 one way, 25 minutes, every half hour) is the quickest way to get to places by Museumplein and Leidseplein. Buses depart from outside the arrivals hall door at platform B17. Buy a ticket from the driver (credit/debit cards only; no cash).

Taxi Taxis take 30 to 45 minutes to the centre (longer in heavy traffic), costing around €50.

The taxi stand is just outside the door of the arrivals hall.

Lelystad Airport

Lelystad Airport (lelystadairport.nl), 50km east of Amsterdam, is undergoing a multimillion-dollar expansion that could see it take on some commercial flights from Schiphol airport. At the time of printing, authorities plan to decide in 2024, and have already delayed the plans several years.

Getting Around

Tram

○ Most public transport within the city is by tram. The vehicles are fast, frequent and ubiquitous, operating between 6am and 12.30am.

○ Tickets are sold on board by credit/debit card only (cash not accepted). Buy a disposable **OV-chipkaart** (ov-chipkaart.nl) (one hour €3.40) or a day pass (one to seven days €9

Tickets & Passes

o Travel passes are extremely handy and provide substantial savings over per-ride ticket purchases.

o The GVB offers unlimited-ride passes for one to seven days (€9 to €41), valid on trams, some buses and the metro.

o Passes are available at the **GVB information office** (gvb.nl) and **I amsterdam Store** (iamsterdam.com), but not on board.

o The I amsterdam Card (per 24/48/72/96/120 hours €60/85/100/115/125) includes a GVB travel pass in its fee.

o A wider-ranging option is the Amsterdam & Region Day Ticket (per one/two/three days €21/31.50/40.50), which goes beyond the tram/metro system, adding on night buses, airport buses, Connexxion buses and regional EBS buses that go to towns such as Haarlem, Muiden and Zaanse Schans. The pass is available at the GVB office and at visitor centres.

o Another choice is the Amsterdam Travel Ticket (per one/two/three days €18/24/30). It's basically a GVB unlimited-ride pass with an airport train ticket added on. Buy it at the airport (at the NS ticket window) or GVB office.

to €41) from the **GVB information office** (gvb.nl).

o When you enter *and* exit, wave your card at the machine to 'check in' and 'check out'.

Metro & Bus

o Prices for the metro and most buses are the same as trams, and use GVB's integrated ticketing system.

o *Nachtbussen* (night buses) run after other transport stops (from 1am to 6am, every hour). A ticket costs €4.50.

o Note that Connexxion buses (which depart from Centraal Station and are useful to reach sights in southern Amsterdam) and the 397 airport bus are not part of the GVB system. They cost more (around €6.50).

Bicycle

o Rental shops are everywhere.

o You'll have to show a passport or European national ID card and leave a credit-card authorisation or pay a deposit (usually €80 to €100).

o Prices per 24-hour period for basic 'coaster-brake' bikes average €16. Bikes with gears and handbrakes cost more. Electric bikes start from €30 for 24 hours.

o Theft insurance (from €3.50 per day) is strongly advised.

o There are a number of bike rental companies, including:

Ajax Bike (ajaxbike.nl) In De Pijp.

Bike City (bikecity.nl) In the Jordaan.

Black Bikes (black-bikes.com) Twenty locations, including in the centre.

Damstraat Rent-a-Bike (rentabike.nl) Near the Dam.

MacBike (macbike.nl) Has a convenient location at Centraal Station, plus others including Waterlooplein and Leidseplein.

Taxi

○ Taxis are expensive and not very speedy given Amsterdam's maze of streets.

○ You don't hail taxis on the road. Instead, find them at stands at Centraal Station, Leidseplein and other busy spots around town. You needn't take the first car in the queue.

○ Another method is to book a taxi by phone. **Amsterdam Taxi Centrale** (amsterdamtaxicentrale.com) is the most reliable company.

○ Fares are meter-based. The meter starts at €3.60, then it's €2.65 per kilometre thereafter. A ride from Leidseplein to the Dam costs about €18; from Centraal Station to the Jordaan is around €22.

○ Uber operates in Amsterdam; rates vary according to demand.

○ Taxi companies are legally obligated to investigate complaints; if they don't, you can complain to the police.

Car

○ Parking is expensive and scarce (and hazardous next to canals).

○ Street parking in the centre costs around €7.50/55 per hour/day.

○ It's better (and cheaper) to leave your vehicle in a park-and-ride lot at the edge of town. See iamsterdam.com for details.

○ All the big multinational rental companies are in town; many have offices on Overtoom, near the Vondelpark.

Train

○ Trains run by **NS** (ns.nl) serve the outer suburbs and, aside from travelling to/from the airport, most visitors to Amsterdam will rarely need to use them unless undertaking trips further afield.

○ Tickets can be bought at the NS service desk

windows or at ticketing machines. The ticket windows are easiest to use, though there is often a queue.

○ Pay with cash, debit or credit card. Visa and MasterCard are accepted, though there is a €0.50 surcharge to use them, and they must have chip-and-PIN technology.

○ There is a €1 surcharge for buying a single-use disposable ticket.

○ Visitors can get a non-personalised rechargeable OV-Chipkaart at NS windows or at GVB public transport offices. It costs €7.50 (non-refundable) and has a €20 minimum balance.

○ You must top up OV-Chipkaarts at NS machines to use NS trains.

Journey Planner

Website **9292.nl** calculates routes, costs and travel times, and will get you from door to door, wherever you're going in the city. The site is in English and Dutch.

Top Navigation Tips

o A *gracht* (canal), such as Egelantiersgracht, is distinct from a *straat* (street) such as Egelantiersstraat.

o A *dwarsstraat* (cross-street) that intersects a *straat* is often preceded by *eerste*, *tweede*, *derde* and *vierde* (first, second, third and fourth; marked 1e, 2e, 3e and 4e on maps). For example, Eerste Egelantiersdwarsstraat is the first cross-street of Egelantiersstraat (ie the nearest cross-street to the city centre).

o Streets preceded by *lange* (long) and *korte* (short) simply mean the longer or shorter street.

o Seemingly continuous streets regularly change name along their length.

o If you want to use a ticketing machine and pay cash, bear in mind that they accept coins only (no paper bills). The machines have instructions in English.

o Check both in *and* out with your ticket/card. Tap it against the card reader in the gates or at freestanding posts.

E-Scooter

Other than private driveways and gardens, e-scooters are banned in the Netherlands. Riding one on public roads and bike lanes is illegal, and will result in a hefty fine.

Essential Information

Accessible Travel

o Travellers with reduced mobility will find Amsterdam moderately equipped to meet their needs.

o Most offices and museums have lifts and/or ramps, and toilets for visitors with disabilities.

o A large number of budget and midrange hotels have limited accessibility, as they occupy old buildings with steep stairs and no lifts.

o Restaurants tend to be on ground floors, though 'ground' sometimes includes a few steps.

o Most buses are wheelchair accessible, as are metro stations. Trams are becoming more accessible as new equipment is added. Many lines have elevated stops for wheelchair users. The website of **GVB** (gvb.nl) denotes which stops are wheelchair accessible.

o A downloadable guide by **Accessible Travel Netherlands** (accessibletravel.nl) shows restaurants, sights, transport and routes in Amsterdam for those with limited mobility.

o A fantastic blog with information about wheelchair-friendly venues and activities is **Able Amsterdam** (ableamsterdam.com)

Business Hours

Opening hours sometimes decrease during off-peak months (October to Easter).

Cafés (pubs), bars & coffeeshops Open noon (exact hours vary); most close 1am Sunday to Thursday, 3am Friday and

Saturday. By law, bars in the Red Light District close at 2am.

General office hours 8.30am–5pm Monday to Friday

Museums 10am–5pm, though some close Monday.

Restaurants 11am–2.30pm and 6–10pm

Shops 9am/10am–6pm Monday to Saturday, noon–6pm Sunday. Smaller shops may keep shorter hours and/or close Monday. Many shops stay open late (to 9pm) Thursday.

Supermarkets 8am–8pm; in the city centre some stay open until 9pm or 10pm.

Discount Cards

I amsterdam Card
(iamsterdam.com) (per 24/48/72/96/120 hours €60/85/100/115/125) Provides admission to more than 30 museums, a canal cruise, and discounts at shops, entertainment venues and restaurants. Also includes a GVB transit pass. Useful for quick visits to the city. Available at the I amsterdam Store, some hotels and online.

Museumkaart
(museumkaart.nl) (adult/child €75/39) Free and discounted entry to some 500 museums all over the country for one year. Purchase it at participating museum ticket counters. You initially receive a temporary card valid for 31 days (maximum five museums); you can then register it online and receive a permanent card sent to a Dutch address, such as your hotel, within three to five working days.

Electricity

Type C
220V/50Hz

Type F
230V/50Hz

Emergencies

Police, fire, ambulance	112
Netherlands country code	31
International access code	00

Money

ATMs

Automatic teller machines can be found outside most banks, at the airport and at Centraal Station. Most accept credit cards such as Visa and MasterCard, as well as cash cards that access the Cirrus and Plus networks. Check with your home bank for

Money-Saving Tips

- Free events and entertainment are plentiful.
- Self-caterers will find numerous parks for picnicking.
- Order the *dagschotel* (dish of the day) or *dagmenu* (set menu of three or more courses) at restaurants.

service charges before leaving.

In the city centre and at the airport, ATMs often have queues or run out of cash on weekends.

Cash

A surprising number of businesses do not accept credit cards, so it's wise to have cash on hand. (Conversely, many places only accept cards.)

Changing Money

Generally your best bet for exchanging money is to use **GWK Travelex** (gwktravelex. nl), which has several branches around town, including GWK Travelex Centraal Station, GWK Travelex Leidseplein and GWK Travelex Schiphol Airport.

Credit Cards

All the major international credit cards are recognised, and most hotels and large stores accept them. But a fair number of shops, restaurants and other businesses, such as some supermarkets, do not accept credit cards, or only accept debit cards with chip-and-PIN technology. Be aware that foreign-issued cards (even chip-and-PIN-enabled foreign credit or debit cards) aren't always accepted (including in some ticket machines), so check first.

Some establishments levy a 5% surcharge (or more) on credit cards to offset the commissions charged by card providers. Always ask beforehand.

Currency

The Netherlands uses the euro (€). Denominations of the currency are €5, €10, €20, €50, €100, €200 and €500 notes, and €0.05, €0.10, €0.20, €0.50, €1 and €2 coins (amounts under €1 are called cents). Unlike many eurozone countries, one- and two-cent coins aren't used in the Netherlands.

Tipping

Bars Not expected.

Hotels Tip €1 to €2 per bag for porters; cleaning staff get a few euros for a job well done.

Restaurants Leave 5% to 10% for a cafe snack (if your bill comes to €9.50, you might round up to €10), 10% or so for a restaurant meal.

Taxis Tip 5% to 10%, or round up to the nearest euro.

Tourist Tax

Amsterdam levies a *toeristenbelasting* (tourist tax) of 12.5% per night, per person for travellers staying overnight in hotels, short-term rentals, B&Bs and camp-grounds, which is added to your bill.

Public Holidays

Most museums adopt Sunday hours on public holidays – and are sometimes even open on Christmas Day and New Year's Day. Check before you go.

Nieuwjaarsdag (New Year's Day) 1 January

Goede Vrijdag (Good Friday) March/April

Eerste Paasdag (Easter Sunday) March/April

Tweede Paasdag (Easter Monday) March/April

Koningsdag (King's Day) 27 April (26 April if 27 April is a Sunday)

Dodenherdenking (Remembrance Day) 4 May (unofficial)

Bevrijdingsdag (Liberation Day) 5 May (unofficially celebrated annually; officially every five years, next in 2025)

Hemelvaartsdag (Ascension Day) 40th day after Easter Sunday

Eerste Pinksterdag (Whit Sunday; Pentecost) 50th day after Easter Sunday

Tweede Pinksterdag (Whit Monday) 50th day after Easter Monday

Eerste Kerstdag (Christmas Day) 25 December

Tweede Kerstdag (Second Christmas; Boxing Day) 26 December

Safe Travel

Amsterdam is a safe and manageable city and if you use your common sense you should have no problems.

○ Stay alert for pickpockets in tourist-heavy zones such as Centraal Station, the Bloemenmarkt and the Red Light District.

○ Avoid deserted streets in the Red Light District at night.

○ It is forbidden to take photos of women in the Red Light District windows; this is strictly enforced.

○ Be careful around the canals. Almost none of

them have fences or barriers.

○ Watch out for bicycles; never walk in bicycle lanes and always look carefully before you cross one.

Toilets

○ Public toilets are not a widespread facility on Dutch streets, apart from the freestanding public urinals for men in places such as the Red Light District.

○ Many people duck into a *café* (pub; ask first!) or department store.

○ The standard fee for toilet attendants is around €1.

○ The app **HogeNood** (High Need; hogenood.nu) maps the nearest toilets based on your location.

Tourist Information

I amsterdam Store (iamsterdam.com) Situated on Centraal Station's northern side, sells tickets to events, tourist passes and Dutch products, and provides basic tourist information.

Dos & Don'ts

Greetings Do give a firm handshake and a double or triple cheek kiss.

Cannabis & alcohol Don't smoke dope or drink beer on the streets.

Smoking Smoking (any substance) in bars or restaurants is illegal.

Bluntness Don't take offence if locals give you a frank, unvarnished opinion. It's not considered impolite, rather it comes from the desire to be direct and honest.

Cycling paths & tram tracks Don't walk in bike lanes (marked by white lines and bicycle symbols) or along tram tracks, and do look both ways before crossing them.

Visas

The Netherlands is part of the Schengen Agreement, which includes all EU states (minus Ireland) and a handful of European countries including Switzerland.

From mid-2025, nationals of some 60 visa-exempt countries – including much of Eastern Europe, Israel, the USA, the UK, Canada, the majority of Central and South American nations, Japan, Malaysia, Singapore, Australia and New Zealand – will need prior authorisation to enter under the European Travel Information and Authorisation System (ETIAS) for stays of up to 90 days within any 180-day period in the Schengen zone. Travellers can apply online; the cost is €7 for multi-entry authorisation for three years or until your travel docu-ment's expiry, whichever comes first. Apply well in advance of your trip. See travel-europe.europa.eu/etias_en for full details.

For citizens of countries requiring ETIAS, and nationals of Ireland, ETIAS pre-authorisation is not required.

Nationals of non-visa-exempt countries, including nationals of China, Russia and South Africa, require a visa. In general, a visa issued by one Schengen country is good for all of the other member countries.

The Netherlands Foreign Affairs Ministry (government.nl) lists consulates and embassies around the world. Visas and extensions are handled by the Immigratie en Naturalisatie dienst (Immigration & Naturalisation Service; ind.nl). Study visas must be applied for via your college or university in the Netherlands.

Language

The pronunciation of Dutch is fairly straightforward. If you read our pronunciation guides as if they were English, you'll be understood just fine. Note that **öy** is pronounced as the 'er y' (without the 'r') in 'her year', and **kh** is a throaty sound, similar to the 'ch' in the Scottish *loch*.

Where relevant, both polite and informal options in Dutch are included, indicated with 'pol' and 'inf', respectively.

To enhance your trip with a phrasebook, visit **lonelyplanet.com**.

Basics

Hello.	*Dag./Hallo.*	*dakh/ha·loh*
Goodbye.	*Dag.*	*dakh*
Yes.	*Ja.*	*yaa*
No.	*Nee.*	*ney*

Please.
Alstublieft. (pol)   *al·stew·bleeft*
Alsjeblieft. (inf)   *a·shuh·bleeft*

Thank you.
Dank u/je. (pol/inf) *dangk ew/yuh*

Excuse me.
Excuseer mij.   *eks·kew·zeyr mey*

How are you?
Hoe gaat het met   *hoo khaat huht met*
u/jou? (pol/inf)   *ew/yaw*

Fine. And you?
Goed. En met   *khoot en met*
u/jou? (pol/inf)   *ew/yaw*

Do you speak English?
Spreekt u Engels?   *spreykt ew eng·uhls*

I don't understand.
Ik begrijp   *ik buh·khreyp*
het niet.   *huht neet*

Eating & Drinking

I'd like ...
Ik wil graag ...   *ik wil khraakh ...*

a beer	*een bier*	*uhn beer*
a coffee	*een koffie*	*uhn ko·fee*
a table for two	*een tafel voor twee*	*uhn taa·fuhl vohr twey*
the menu	*een menu*	*uhn me·new*

I don't eat (meat).
Ik eet geen (vlees). *ik eyt kheyn (vleys)*

Delicious!
Heerlijk!/Lekker!   *heyr·luhk/le·kuhr*

Cheers!
Proost!   *prohst*

Please bring the bill.
Mag ik de   *makh ik duh*
rekening   *rey·kuh·ning*
alstublieft?   *al·stew·bleeft*

Shopping

I'd like to buy ...
Ik wil graag ...   *ik wil khraakh ...*
kopen.   *koh·puhn*

I'm just looking.
Ik kijk alleen maar. *ik keyk a·leyn maar*

How much is it?
Hoeveel kost het?   *hoo·veyl kost huht*

That's too expensive.
Dat is te duur.   *dat is tuh dewr*

Can you lower the price?
Kunt u wat van   *kunt ew wat van*
de prijs afdoen?   *duh preys af·doon*

Emergencies

Help!
Help!   *help*

Call a doctor!
Bel een dokter!   *bel uhn dok·tuhr*

Call the police!
Bel de politie!   *bel duh poh·leet·see*

I'm sick.
Ik ben ziek.   *ik ben zeek*

I'm lost.
Ik ben verdwaald.   *ik ben vuhr·dwaalt*

Where are the toilets?
Waar zijn de   *waar zeyn duh*
toiletten?   *twa·le·tuhn*

Time & Numbers

What time is it?
Hoe laat is het?   *hoo laat is huht*

It's (10) o'clock.
Het is (tien) uur.   *huht is (teen) ewr*

Half past (10).
Half (elf).   *half (elf)*
(lit: half eleven)

morning	's ochtends	sokh·tuhns
afternoon	's middags	smi·dakhs
evening	's avonds	saa·vonts

yesterday	gisteren	khis·tuh·ruhn
today	vandaag	van·daakh
tomorrow	morgen	mor·khuhn

1	één	eyn
2	twee	twey
3	drie	dree
4	vier	veer
5	vijf	veyf
6	zes	zes
7	zeven	zey·vuhn
8	acht	akht
9	negen	ney·khuhn
10	tien	teen

Transport & Directions

Where's the ...?
Waar is ...?   *waar is ...*

How far is it?
Hoe ver is het?   *hoo ver is huht*

What's the address?
Wat is het adres?   *wat is huht a·dres*

Can you show me (on the map)?
Kunt u het mij   *kunt ew huht mey*
tonen (op de   *toh·nuhn (op duh*
kaart)?   *kaart)*

A ticket to ..., please.
Een kaartje naar   *uhn kaar·chuh naar*
..., graag.   *... khraakh*

Please take me to ...
Breng me   *breng muh*
alstublieft   *al·stew·bleeft*
naar ...   *naar ...*

Does it stop at ...?
Stopt het in ...?   *stopt huht in ...*

I'd like to get off at ...
Ik wil graag in ...   *ik wil khraak in ...*
uitstappen.   *öyt·sta·puhn*

Can we get there by bike?
Kunnen we er   *ku·nuhn wuh uhr*
met de fiets heen?   *met duh feets heyn*

Behind the Scenes

Send Us Your Feedback

We love to hear from travellers – your comments help make our books better. We read every word, and we guarantee that your feedback goes straight to the authors. Visit **lonelyplanet.com/contact** to submit your updates and suggestions.

Note: We may edit, reproduce and incorporate your comments in Lonely Planet products such as guidebooks, websites and digital products, so let us know if you are happy to have your name acknowledged. For a copy of our privacy policy visit lonelyplanet.com/legal.

Catherine's Thanks

Hartelijk bedankt first and foremost to Julian, and to everyone in Amsterdam and beyond who provided insights, inspiration and good times during this update and over the years. Huge thanks too to Destination Editor Sandie Kestell and everyone at LP. As ever, eternal love to my family.

Acknowledgements

Front cover photograph: Sluishuis (p160, architects: BIG – Bjarke Ingels Group); biletskiyevgeniy.com/Shutterstock ©

Back cover photograph: Sergey Bezgodov/Shutterstock ©

This Book

This 9th edition of Lonely Planet's *Pocket Amsterdam* guidebook was researched and written by Catherine Le Nevez. The previous edition was written by Barbara Woolsey.

This guidebook was produced by the following:

Destination Editor
Sandie Kestell

Product Editor
Hannah Cartmel

Cartographer
Julie Sheridan

Book Designer
Aomi Ito

Assisting Editors
Kellie Langdon, Clifton Wilkinson

Cover Researcher
Kat Marsh

Thanks to Ronan Abayawickrema, Doc O'Connell, Charlotte Orr, Vicky Smith

Index

See also separate subindexes for:

⊗ **Eating p188**

Ⓓ **Drinking p189**

☆ **Entertainment p190**

🔒 **Shopping p190**

Our Writer

Catherine Le Nevez

Writing for Lonely Planet since 2004, Catherine has authored, researched and curated well over 100 guidebooks and Trade & Reference titles for destinations worldwide, along with numerous digital articles and photography. Catherine's travels have taken her to some 60 countries, completing her Doctorate of Creative Arts in Writing, Masters in Professional Writing, and postgrad qualifications in Editing and Publishing along the way. Wanderlust aside, Amsterdam remains one of her all-time favourite cities on Earth.

Published by Lonely Planet Global Limited
CRN 554153
9th edition – June 2024
ISBN 978 1 83869 867 6
© Lonely Planet 2024   Photographs © as indicated 2024
10 9 8 7 6 5 4 3 2 1
Printed in Malaysia